A Pope and a Council
on the Sacred Liturgy

A Pope and a Council on the Sacred Liturgy

Pope Pius XII's *Mediator Dei*
and the Second Vatican Council's
Sacrosanctum Concilium
with a comparative study
"A Tale of Two Documents"
by Aidan Nichols OP

Saint Michael's Abbey Press
MMII

SAINT MICHAEL'S ABBEY PRESS
Saint Michael's Abbey
Farnborough
Hants. GU14 7NQ

Telephone +44 (0) 1252 546 105
Facsimile +44 (0) 1252 372 822

www.farnboroughabbey.org
prior@farnboroughabbey.org

ISBN 0 907077 38 2

Printed and bound in Great Britain by Biddles Ltd,
Guildford and King's Lynn.

Table of Contents

Preface

One cannot underestimate the importance of *Mediator Dei*. Dom Lambert Beauduin OSB, father of the twentieth century Liturgical Movement, asserted that it was:

> A solemn, unique document by which the supreme authority rehabilitates the Liturgy – yesterday's Cinderella – in its rights and claims of primacy. To be sure, Popes Pius X and Pius XI had spoken decisive words, but our Holy Father Pius XII is the first to explain in a magisterial document, vibrant with apostolic ardour, the basic prerogatives which entitle the Liturgy to a post of the first order in the spiritual life.[1]

The Liturgical Movement's North American journal, *Orate Fratres*, was grateful that the movement "finally has been granted official Catholic status,"[2] and declared that it had "come of age."[3] The 1948 North American Liturgical Week was told that "*Mediator Dei* is a beacon light. It makes the liturgical endeavour now not a matter of choice but a *must*, an apostolate incumbent upon all."[4] Yet, as the official summary issued by the Secretariat of State indicates, the purpose of the encyclical was also to "restrain the imprudent."[5]

Just over sixteen years elapsed between November 20th, 1947, when Pope Pius XII signed *Mediator Dei,* and December 4th, 1963, when the Second Vatican Council approved *Sacrosanctum Concilium*; sixteen years of unparalleled activity in the history of reform in the Roman rite. In them, whilst promoting liturgical

---

[1] "L'Encyclique *Mediator Dei*" in *La Maison-Dieu*, no. 13, p. 7.
[2] "Liturgical Briefs" *Orate Fratres* vol. XXII p. 90.
[3] "Liturgical Briefs" *Orate Fratres* vol. XXII p. 139.
[4] John E. Kelly, "The Encyclical, *Mediator Dei*" in: *The New Man in Christ: National Liturgical Week 1948*, The Liturgical Conference, Conception, Mo., 1949, p. 11.
[5] "Mediator Dei" in *The Tablet* vol. 190, p. 359.

spirituality, the Liturgical Movement's activists studied, debated, proposed, and in some cases agitated for reform.

Few who read *Mediator Dei* upon publication could have imagined the reforms that ensued. None imagined that within twenty years an ecumenical council would call for a general reform of the Sacred Liturgy.

Few who read *Sacrosanctum Concilium* in 1964 expected the rapid, numerous, and not insubstantial changes that would be made to the Roman rite in the subsequent years. Rather, they saw the Liturgical Movement as having "reached its maturity."[6]

Today, the identification of the ideals of the Liturgical Movement with these changes is questioned. The authoritative and seminal texts in this volume,[7] and the incisive comparative study of Father Aidan Nichols OP, are published here to assist and to inform contemporary debate about twentieth century liturgical reform.

Alcuin Reid
Palm Sunday, 2002

---

[6] Archbishop Paul Hallinan, "The Church's Liturgy: Growth and Development," in: *The Challenge of the Council: Person, Parish World – Twenty-Fifth North American Liturgical Week, St Louis 1964*, The Liturgical Conference, Washington, D.C., 1964, p. 95.

[7] With acknowledgement to the Holy See for the translations of *Mediator Dei* and *Sacrosanctum Concilium*. Latin texts: cf. C. Braga & A. Bugnini, eds., *Documenta Ad Instaurationem Liturgicam Spectantia 1903-1963*, Centro Liturgico Vincenziano, Rome, 2000; and: R. Kaczynski, ed., *Enchiridion Documentorum Instaurationis Liturgicæ I (1963-1973)*, Marietti, 1976.

A Tale of Two Documents:
Sacrosanctum Concilium and *Mediator Dei*[1]

Aidan Nichols, O.P.

The semi-centenary of Pope Pius XII's 1947 encyclical *Mediator Dei*, once hailed as the "charter" of the Liturgical Movement, came and went in 1997 with no great brouhaha. Yet in seeking a title for an essay comparing that letter with the now much more celebrated *Sacrosanctum Concilium* of Vatican II issued in 1963, I put the name of the Conciliar Liturgy Constitution before that of the 1947 document almost entirely for reasons of euphony. For not only chronologically but also in terms of theological substance — at any rate in most if not in all respects, as I hope to show — the primacy belongs to *Mediator Dei*. In saying as much, I am no doubt condemning myself in some Catholic quarters (does not *Mediator Dei* represent the closed world of the last of the Pian popes, from which we were graciously emancipated by Vatican II?), just as I am simultaneously endearing myself in others (was not *Sacrosanctum Concilium*, through the liturgical revolution it unleashed, the cause, in the area of worship, of our present woes?). The way we look back at these two major documents of twentieth-century Catholicism can hardly be unaffected by how we evaluate the postconciliar epoch in the Catholic Church both in general and in the specifically liturgical domain.

Here the opening words of Charles Dickens' *A Tale of Two Cities* are surely apposite. Summing up the wildly conflicting judgements by contemporaries on the revolutionary events initiated by the summoning of the Estates-General in France, Dickens wrote:

It was the best of times, it was the worst of times, it was the age of wisdom, it was the age of foolishness, it was the epoch of

---

[1] An earlier version of this essay was published in *Antiphon* 5:1 (2000), pp. 23-31.

belief, it was the epoch of incredulity, it was the season of Light, it was the season of Darkness.[2]

Dickens himself, as the ironic tone of this passage suggests, believed the revolutionary period to be neither. What he *did* believe about it I shall return to at the close of my analysis—for the analogy between the Great Revolution of the West and the ecclesial revolution of the last generation is not without value. For the moment, however, we can register the fact, echoing Dickens' overture, that, for the historian, the likelihood that *any* time in the Church's life is nothing but light celestial is as great as the likelihood that any time in the Church's history is made up of unremitting gloom—which is to say that the likelihood is very small indeed. My contention that *Mediator Dei* (hereafter *MD*) is, in most aspects, a more substantial document than *Sacrosanctum Concilium* (hereafter *SC*) is founded not on *a priori* preference for things preconciliar, but rather on exploration of the well-foundedness and adequacy of the ideas of Pius' encyclical.

Before embarking on an exposition of those ideas, and indeed of the smaller set represented by the Conciliar Constitution as well, one caveat, already hinted at, should be stressed, and two others should be entered.

Caveat One: Theological

In one major respect I find the theology of the Liturgy in *SC* to enjoy a distinct advantage over the understanding of worship in *MD*, and that is in its more pronounced orientation towards the *eschaton*, the Lord's *Parousia* at the end of time. This theme is almost entirely absent from Pius XII's encyclical, and even now is still hardly central, despite the Conciliar Constitution, to the liturgical consciousness of Western Catholics using the reformed rites. Eschatological consciousness is highly conspicuous, not to say the predominant consideration, in what is perhaps the most impressive, if little noticed, theology of the

---

[2] Charles Dickens, *A Tale of Two Cities*, chapter one, 1.

Liturgy produced in the present pontificate by an author, later commissioned (and not accidentally) to write the concluding book of the 1992 Catechism of the Catholic Church, the section on prayer.[3]

Caveat Two: Literary-Historical

In terms of modern Catholicism's history, it is perfectly defensible to say that, when we compare *SC* with *MD* we are not, strictly speaking, comparing like with like. The two documents do not belong to the same genre. In saying that, I do not have in mind the fact that one is conciliar and the other papal in its formal authority. My point has to do with the kind of text that the authors envisaged. Pius XII intended to offer an evaluation of the Liturgical Movement of his time by painting a doctrinal portrait of what the Sacred Liturgy is. He proposed to set forth what was salutary, as distinct from what was either exaggerated or defective about that movement, by providing a fully rounded picture of the Liturgy in terms of theological doctrine. Pius aimed to correct certain distortions in people's minds, as well as abuses in the manner of liturgical celebration, by giving a theologically true account of the nature of Christian worship. His intervention, we can say, was essentially theoretical, though it had, to be sure, a practical finality.

The fathers of the Second Vatican Council, by contrast, intended to provide guidelines for an imminent reform of the liturgical books and a reformulation of liturgical law. To this end they evidently thought it sufficient to preface their practical proposals with a relatively brief theological prologue, though they also reverted on occasion to wider doctrinal considerations when introducing particular topics of reform: the rite of the Mass, the Church calendar, the Divine Office. Accordingly, we can say that the intervention of the bishops at Vatican II was essentially practical, though they bore in mind certain theoretical principles. Evidently, one cannot criticise *SC* for not fulfilling a promise the

---

[3] Jean Corbon, *The Wellspring of Worship* (Mahwah, N.J., Paulist Press, 1988).

fathers of Vatican II never gave. Yet with the benefit of hindsight, one could regret that the predominantly practical character of their proposals, made as these were in a culturally pragmatist age, was not balanced in advance by a fuller theology of worship, drawing not least on *MD*.

Caveat Three: Political-Pastoral

The final caveat I would register against my thesis is that the contrast between the two documents should not be exploited polemically, creating conflict, *polemos*, by setting one at the throat of the other. The difference between *MD* and *SC* is, to revert to the Dickens comparison, not the difference between Louis XIV and Robespierre. At the most it is the difference between Cardinal Richelieu and the Constituent Assembly. Or, to put the point less allusively — in terms of the spectrum of opinion about the Liturgy in their periods (the 1940's and the 1960's respectively) — *MD* is set against a background of liturgical conservatism, much of it by inertia, and is a moderately reformist document — though, as we shall see, it contains the ingredients of a recipe for a neo-orthodox reaction to liturgical reform. *SC* is set against a background of growing liturgical radicalism and is a largely traditional document — though at the same time it carried within it, encased in the innocuous language of pastoral welfare, some seeds of its own destruction.

An 'Ordo Expositionis'

In this essay I shall concentrate on *three main differences* in the conception of the Liturgy stated or implicit in *SC* and *MD*. These are: first, the role of a theology of devotion — what Pius XII's encyclical calls the primacy of "internal worship;" second, the principle stated therein that all liturgical ages of the New Testament Church, and not simply that of the primitive development of the rites, are open to God; and third — and this is the point on which I hold *MD* to be *inferior* to *SC*, the exclusively realised eschatology invoked by the papal letter to describe the ultimate reality we encounter in the liturgical action. *MD* views that more-than-human reality made available in the Sacred Liturgy — and *rendering* it sacred, indeed — as the *present* most holy being of Jesus Christ, the God-man, in the fullness of his saving activity for us. But this is at the expense of a sense of the Liturgy as the realised anticipation of the future *Parousia* of the Lord — his coming with all his saints to inaugurate the final plenitude which that all-sufficient saving activity makes possible: the reign of the Father in the Holy Spirit — not the new heavens only, which we have already through the access of those redeemed by Christ to the Beatific Vision, but also the new earth.

Exposition of those three main points must, however, be topped and tailed. I shall *round them off* by drawing attention to two other less structural but by no means unimportant differences of emphasis between the two documents. But beforehand, I want to *preface* them by mentioning one enormous fact which the two texts have in common and which alone, despite the discontinuities they may contain, sets them aside from many alternative statements of the rationale of worship available in today's Church: that is the *soteriological perspective* in which they see all liturgical action, the way they treat the Liturgy as essentially in function of *Christian salvation*.

To elaborate: Both *SC*, after an initial paragraph outlining why a Council with the aims which Vatican II set itself should be concerned with the Liturgy at all, and *MD* from the very outset, furnish a rationale for liturgical celebration which is entirely salvational in character. Far from providing an explanation of why there is a Liturgy couched in terms of sociology, religious philosophy, or political ethics — all of which could well have predominated in subsequent discussion — both documents begin by asserting that the Liturgy only makes sense in relation to salvation. In the 1947 papal letter, it is by the Liturgy especially that "the Church at the bidding of her Founder continues the priestly office of Jesus Christ,"[4] a priestly office undertaken, so

---

[4] *Mediator Dei*, no. 3 [3]. Text from *Mediator Dei* (London: Catholic Truth Society, 1960). [The Latin original does not number the paragraphs.

the pope explained, in order to "re-establish between men and their Creator the order that sins had upset and so bring back to their heavenly Father, first beginning and last end of all creatures, the unhappy progeny of Adam."[5] The sacrifice of the altar, the sacraments, and the Liturgy of the Hours considered (and here the twelfth Pius quoted the eleventh) as expressive of the thanksgiving, praise, petition and expiation prayed by Christ's own mystical Body, prolong the self-offering of the incarnate Word by which, when on earth, he set the sinful on the way of return to the Father. These sacred actions carry, then, a supreme significance for our salvation, enabling believers — in the words of that crucial opening paragraph of the letter — to co-operate "personally in their sanctification, making their own the holiness that springs from the blood of the unspotted Lamb."[6] That notion of personal co-operation (what the Greek Fathers call *synergia*, co-working), whereby one must make a spiritual effort in the Liturgy congruent with God's outreach in sacred signs, will be highly relevant to what I have called Pius XII's "theology of devotion."

Just the same salvational perspective, seeing the Liturgy as the continuing expression of the Father's offer to us of new holiness through the sacrificial death of Christ, is also the burden of the early sections of *SC*. In fact, the doctrinal link between the Liturgy and salvation is, if anything, tightened in those early paragraphs of the Liturgy Constitution, by citation of a "Secret" prayer for the time after Pentecost which states that, through the Liturgy, *opus nostræ Redemptionis exercetur* ("the work of our redemption is carried on").[7] In both documents, then, we are worlds away from any sub-theological ideology of the Liturgy for which the purpose of the Liturgy might be, for instance, to affirm the group identity of the assembly; to express gender, class or ethnic belonging; or to recognise in symbolic play the presence or

---

References to paragraph numbers used in the translation published in this volume are given in square brackets.]

[5] Ibid., no. 1 [1].

[6] Ibid.

[7] *Sacrosanctum Concilium,* no. 2; see no. 6. Text from W. M. Abbott, *The Documents of Vatican II* (London and Dublin: Geoffrey Chapman, 1966).

action of the divine in secular life and reality. There are, no doubt, legitimate senses in which the Liturgy might be said, incidentally and *per accidens,* to perform some or, on occasion, even all of these job descriptions, but none of these gets anywhere near stating what the essential rationale of the Liturgy is.

MD and *SC* come identifiably then from the same stable; or, to put the point in more theological language: both are recognisable expressions of the doctrine of worship which has always been implicit in the faith of the Church.

Difference One: Doing Justice to Devotion

Let us consider now the chief points of difference in this tale of two documents. The first two aspects, in which *MD* scores well when compared with its successor text, is what I have termed the "theology of devotion." This theme plays a crucial part in the way Pius XII saw liturgical participation as offering us the opportunity for *synergia*, co-working, with the protagonist of our salvation, the immaculate Lamb. How did this theology of devotion come to enter Pius XII's thoughts, or those of his counsellors, on this subject? It appears to have been a reaction to "hyper-liturgists" who, beginning in the late 1920's, took to an extreme the emphasis on the priority of the Liturgy in all its objectivity over devotions with all their possible subjectivism. This approach was characteristic of the Benedictine school of Maria Laach. Historically, the contours of the relation between the *Laacher Schule,* as represented by its outstanding scholar-thinker Odo Casel, and the encyclical *MD*, are tricky to plot. Casel and his confrères at first reacted enthusiastically to the papal letter which they hailed as the vindication of precisely that view of the Liturgy which they had worked to establish or re-establish in the Church: mysteric, the action of Christ as the Head in his mystical body, bringing his saving actions to bear in post-Ascension time. But they were soon obliged to heed other voices which declared that *MD*, far from vindicating the monks of Laach, was precisely a condemnation of the "Rhenish innovators." Odo Casel himself died in March 1948 before having the opportunity to clear his name—though in other respects electing the moment of his *transitus* with an impeccable sense for liturgical timing; for he expired during the Paschal vigil acting as deacon, in between the proclamation of *Lumen Christi* and the singing of the *Exsultet*.

An attempt to secure from the Holy Office, via the sympathetic Archbishop of Salzburg, a formal statement that Casel's theology was not being criticised produced only ambiguous results. In Rome, the emphasis on the unique status of liturgical prayer—a common theme of Prosper Guéranger at Solesmes, the Wolter brothers at Beuron, and the Beuron daughter house at Laach was welcomed. But it was not intended that this emphasis should be so presented as to leave no space for the operation of a personal spirituality, no room for the subject's spiritual effort of a wider and more diffuse, if also more personal, and in that sense, more concentrated kind. Though this was not the only perilous tendency the pope saw in certain manifestations of the Liturgical Movement, it is the one to which he gave the maximum attention. The second chapter of the letter is devoted exclusively to the false antinomy, as Pius XII called it, between "objective" and "personal" devotion, and his insistence that subjective devotion is not only helpful but necessary if the Liturgy (including the sacraments, and above all the Mass) is to be of full effect in worshippers' lives. At Laach itself, abbot and monks rallied to the view that any contrary opinions could be ascribed to Casel only by eisegesis, a reading back of them into his texts.

With all due respect to Casel, without whose work much of *MD*'s explanation of the special status of liturgical prayer would be if not unthinkable then at any rate far less readily thinkable, it must be confessed that he did occasionally provide rather large hooks on which anti-devotional interpretations of liturgical assistance could be hung. For instance, in his most widely read book, *Das christliche Kultmysterium* published in 1932 and translated into English in the year the Second Vatican Council opened, Casel is engaged on a comparison between prayer in the ancient Church and prayer in later Christendom, to the detriment of the latter. Prayer, he laments,

Has been moving away from consciousness of the mystical body of Christ, falling into the isolated feeling and thinking of the "God-seeking" individual...The mystery itself, with its objective ordering of things according to God and real union with him disappeared beneath a mass of more or less devotional exercises which left more freedom to individual. *Devotio*, a word which to the ancients meant the Church's worship, became the devotion of a purely interior state of individual consciousness.[8]

One can easily imagine the alarm bells which unilateral interpretation of such a passage sounded in papal ears. The prospect which appalled was not that of a Mass where no one said the rosary. The encyclical is, in fact, quite judicious in the way it exhorts pastors to encourage the fitting of such "devotions" — in the plural — to the liturgical seasons: the sorrowful mysteries during Mass at Passiontide, and, presumably the glorious ones at the Masses of Easter. The prospect, rather, was of a Liturgy which could presume no devotion save that which the last celebration of the Liturgy attended had managed to generate: a Mass, in other words, at which people might well arrive as *tabula rasæ*, blackboards scrubbed clean of any evangelical writing because the wider, personal spiritual effort which the Liturgy presupposes had not been made. There appeared to be an unawareness of any need for preparation for holy communion or thanksgiving after it other than that provided by the "objective" Liturgy — the texts read out by the celebrant in the people's name. Eventually, this prospect was mercifully shielded from the papal gaze! — this could and would lead to churches where as a result of incessant chatter the basic physical conditions for recollectedness in approaching the eucharistic Lord and spending time with him afterwards in prayerful union were in any case no longer met.

Pius XII's theology of devotion in *MD* was intended to close the crack thus opening up between the celebration of the rites, on the one hand, and the ascetical and mystical tradition of personal prayer in the Church, on the other. Basically, Pius takes

---

[8] Odo Casel, *The Mystery of Christian Worship* (London: Darton, Longman and Todd, 1962), 36.

St Thomas's teaching on the virtue of religion (that aspect of justice, our response to what is due, which governs our relations with God) and links this virtue, following Thomas, both to holiness, on the one hand, and to the idea of devotion, on the other. The pope then applies this complex of concepts to making good the gap in the Christian approach to worship which "hyper-liturgism" had caused. Finding the origins of the word "religion" in the verb *religare*, "to bind," Aquinas had described the religious relationship as one in which we should be "bound to God as our unfailing principle," the Alpha of our lives, and "unfailingly choose him as our last end," our Omega.[9] In this sense, Thomas goes on to explain, religion is only notionally distinct from holiness. The word "religion" focuses attention on our taking part in cultic acts expressive of our bond with God; the word "holiness" connotes a wider range of actions relevant to other virtues — all of which, however (and this is the capital point) have the effect of disposing us the better to divine worship.[10] In this — and here I am following the relevant section of the *Summa Theologiæ* (entitled in the Cambridge translation, significantly, "Religion and Worship") more uninterruptedly than did the pope — a special place must be given to that quality of acting Thomas calls "devotion" and which he defines as a willing promptness to do everything that God's service requires, caused, he goes on to explain, by contemplation of and meditation on the divine goodness and mercy to which we are, in turn, moved principally by prayerful consideration of the Passion of Christ.[11] That is why, for Thomas the chief effect of devotion is *spiritualis laetitia mentis*, the "spiritual joy of mind," while its secondary effect is *tristitia secundum Deum*, a specifically divine "sadness" or "sorrow" through an awareness of our own deficiencies.[12]

All spiritualities in the Church may be appropriately regarded as so many different ways of presenting and interrelating those two fundamental kinds of pathos: Christian joy and Christian sorrow. We can note, for instance, how a

---

[9] Thomas Aquinas, *Summa Theologiæ*, IIa. IIae., q. 80, 1.

[10] Ibid., q. 82, 8.

[11] Ibid., q. 82, 3.

[12] Ibid., q. 82, 4.

classical spiritual theologian like Teresa of Avila regards the Sacred Liturgy as a highly congruent setting for the kind of contemplative union which, when they reach their deepest, these attitudes empower. The need to marry the objective texts and gestures of the Liturgy to ascetical and mystical effort along these lines was a salutary preoccupation of Pius XII, albeit one forced upon him, or so it would seem, by the *Mysterienkontroverse*, the debate over Maria Laach's theology of the mysteries, in inter-war German Catholicism.

It is rarely the way of the Roman church to leave historical baggage entirely behind and, once in possession of this background, we can find in paragraphs 11 and 12 of *SC* reference, albeit discreet, to this requirement. This throws considerable light on the most disputed question in the interpretation of the Conciliar Constitution, namely, what it intends by the phrase "active" or "engaged" participation, *actuosa participatio*. What that knotty term *actuosa* means—at any rate in this section of the Constitution—is governed by the theme of the section: the necessity for "right dispositions of the soul," *recti animi dispositiones*—*SC*'s version of the true devotion of *MD*. "Active participation" means primarily contemplatively engaged participation, not jumping up and down, which is why section 30 of the Liturgy Constitution can include silence under this heading.

Difference Two: Honouring History

The devotion theme is, then, not so much entirely absent in *SC* as it is rather thoroughly submerged there. A clearer contrast between the two documents emerges when we consider the second of my claims for the relative superiority of *MD*. This concerns the need to respect the Liturgy's previous history—and this is not so unrelated a theme to the one just investigated as might at first sight seem the case. Though *SC* defends the role in the Liturgy of what it terms "sound tradition," *sana traditio*,[13] it

---

[13] *SC*, no. 23.

largely envisages a retrenchment of the Roman rite to what was, as it puts it, "in vigour in the time of the holy fathers,"[14] *ad pristinam sanctorum Patrum normam*. Just what constitutes the ending of the patristic age has never been fully determined by the Church's divines. Yet, once combined with the somewhat Genevan emphasis in the adjacent clauses of the Constitution on simplification of the rites (though with care not to eviscerate their substance), and the discarding of duplications or possibly superfluous late additions to the Liturgy, this reference to the period of the Fathers served to provide a normative standard for liturgical reform. This suggested strongly to the scholars and administrators to whom the task fell of realising these recommendations in practice, that what was envisaged was not the confluence of the primitive Roman with the more florid Frankish or Gallican Liturgy of the *last* centuries of the first millennium—that synthesis which in fact produced the Roman synthesis of the Middle Ages and the Tridentine reform. What was envisaged rather was the excision, wherever possible, of what did not belong, rather, to the Roman rite of the *first* centuries of that millennium.

Significantly, the Liturgy Constitution of the Council and the establishment of the *consilium* for effecting its proposals which soon followed belong to a time when, in academic liturgiology, an ecumenical consensus reigned about the all-sufficiency of the third century Liturgy—that common "shape," as the Anglican liturgiologist Gregory Dix called it, which typified all the rites, Western and Eastern. Only much more recently has the view become widespread—it is strongly urged, for instance, by Dix's fellow Anglican Paul Bradshaw, now professor of Liturgy at the University of Notre Dame in Indiana—that too much sanitisation has been carried out, both by scholars claiming to detect in very disparate materials a primitive common form, and, what is more to our purposes, by liturgical reformers attempting to prune away whatever is particular in the growth of the Liturgy in later times.

The relevance of this matter to the devotion theme should become clear by reference to an encomium of the historic

---

[14] Ibid., no. 50.

Dominican rite made by the liturgical historian William Bonniwell some two years before *MD*. Praising the mid-thirteenth century revision of that rite by Humbert of Romans as "a masterpiece surpassed by no other rite in the Latin church," Bonniwell explained that he was speaking of the qualities of the developed western Liturgy of the high middle ages: "the ancient Roman qualities of simplicity, dignity and practicality *enriched by a warmer devotion and by a restrained dramatic element so appealing to human nature.*"[15] The post-Vatican II stripping away of various ceremonies and the more devotional non-Roman prayers as unnecessary post-patristic accretions undermined the capacity of the reformed Roman Liturgy to sustain that devotional atmosphere which was needed if the "right dispositions of soul" desiderated by the Liturgy Constitution were to endure, never mind to be brought more fully into play. Such truncation of the Liturgy was exactly what *MD* (noting that the early Fathers had no exclusive monopoly on the best tunes) had tried to prevent. Stigmatising the desire for such drastic pruning as the consequence of "archaeologism," the pope warned that while "to go back in mind and heart to the sources of the Sacred Liturgy is wise and praiseworthy...the desire to restore everything indiscriminately to its ancient condition is neither."[16] The reason is that, just as with the development of doctrine, a Catholic Christian does not maintain that divine guidance left the Church to her own devices after the death of the last of the Fathers, so here too, the post-patristic evolution of the Liturgy cannot be regarded as outside God's providence—cannot be written off as certainly not the result of divine graces working on the corporate imagination of the Church. The attempt of so highly placed a Roman liturgist today as Adrian Nocent to take to a logical conclusion the "demedievalisation" (to coin a phrase) of the Roman rite undertaken by the postconcilar *consilium* through abolishing remaining elements of post-patristic practice, such as the elevation after the consecration of the host and chalice, shows how deeply rooted is a prejudice in matters of the Liturgy which,

---

[15] William R. Bonniwell, *A History of the Dominican Liturgy, 1215-1945* (New York: Wagner, 1945), 193; emphasis added.
[16] *MD*, no. 66 [62].

were it transferred to the field of doctrine, would immediately identify one as un-Catholic in a fundamental sense.

Difference Three: Preparing the Parousia

Let us now tip the scales a little the other way as I move on to my third principal disparity of theological substance in this tale of two documents — this time to the credit of *SC* rather than *MD*. The question of the unique ontological status of the Liturgy is the question of what befalls the prayers we use in church — prayers, most of them, not directly biblical in origin and so the result, primarily, of human creativity rather than divine inspiration — when we deploy those prayers in a strictly liturgical fashion. In what way is the standing of those prayers altered? We do not say of them as we say of the Scriptures, *verbum Domini*, "The Word of the Lord." The answer of *MD* is that these prayers are taken up into the relation which, since the time of Christ's saving historical acts, holds good between the Church, his mystical Body, and himself, the Church's Head, and consequently, since he is in his own person the God-man, the divine-human mediator, into that eternally actual dialogue which unites the Son with the Father. As Pius XII put it:

The Sacred Liturgy is…the public worship which our Redeemer, the Head of the Church, offers the heavenly Father and which the community of Christ's faithful pays to its founder, and through him, to the eternal Father; briefly, it is the whole public worship of the Mystical Body of Jesus Christ, Head and members.[17]

This is why the Liturgy has such dignity, significance, efficacy — why it is, precisely, the *sacred* Liturgy. Pius XII had gone on record in the encyclical as singling out the special debt of the universal Church to that understanding of the Liturgy pioneered by the revived Benedictinism of the nineteenth and

---

[17] Ibid., no. 20 [20].

twentieth centuries. Pius refers to "the devoted zeal of certain monasteries of the renowned Benedictine order."[18] If we were to look for the theological sources of his ontology of the Liturgy we need search no further than, on the one hand, the Solesmes of Guéranger, and, on the other, the Maria Laach of Casel (to whom, as I have stressed the encyclical has a complex relation of attraction and repulsion). Here, for instance, is what Guéranger states in the general preface to the *Année liturgique*:

> Jesus Christ himself is…the means as well as the object of the Liturgy, and that is why the "Year of the Church" we propose to set forth in this work is nothing other than the manifestation of Jesus Christ and of his mysteries in the Church and in the faithful soul…If each year the Church renews her youth "like the eagle's," this is because, through the liturgical cycle, she is visited by her Spouse according to the proportion of her needs. Each year she sees him an infant in the crib, fasting on the mountain, offering himself on the Cross, rising again from the tomb, founding his Church and instituting his sacraments, ascending once more to the Father's right, sending out his Spirit to men; and the graces of these divine mysteries are in turn renewed in the Church in such a fashion that, rendered fertile as need suggests, the garden of the Church sends up to her Spouse at all times [here Guéranger cites the *Song of Solomon*] "by the breath of the North Wind and the South the sweet fragrance of her perfumes."[19]

However, Pius XII's formulation of the relation between the Liturgy and Christ in his mysteries actually rises beyond this, in section 176 [165] of *MD*, wherein the pope speaks, in terms more redolent of Casel, of the liturgical year as being in its inmost reality, *Christus ipse, qui in sua Ecclesia perseverat*, "Christ himself, living in his Church." Human beings may encounter his mysteries and not just—we may gloss the text as saying—their fruits or the graces that flow from them. We encounter the mysteries as they are in themselves and *per eadem quodammodo*

---

[18] Ibid., no. 5 [4].
[19] Dom Prosper Guéranger, "Préface générale," *L'Année liturgique. Avent* (Tours: Mame, 1920), xix, citing *Song of Solomon* 4, 17.

23

viverent, "in a certain sense live by means of them." For what is this save Casel's view that the Liturgy in its total unfolding in the Church's year makes present not just the effects of Christ's redeeming work, from Annunciation to glorification, but Christ himself *in* those redemptive actions still as fully actual as they ever were in history but given to human beings again—indeed, again and again—*sacramentally*, through the mediation of the sacred signs.

For Pope Pius, as for Guéranger at Solesmes and Casel at Laach (and here we might usefully note a third possible Benedictine source midway, in time and space, between these two—Columba Marmion at Maredsous), the Liturgy is the rendering actual in present time of a *past* reality—albeit one that, because of its unique divine-human quality, is not simply past but held in God's eternity. However, there is little or nothing in *MD* about the Liturgy as more than Christological remembrance—as Christological anticipation of *a future yet to come*. This explains no doubt why the encyclical's theology of the Advent season is so disappointingly moralistic and jejune.[20] Here is where *SC* helpfully enters in, to complete the picture. The Vatican II document declares:

> In the earthly Liturgy we take part in a foretaste of that heavenly Liturgy which is celebrated in the holy city of Jerusalem towards which we journey as pilgrims...we eagerly await our Saviour, the Lord Jesus Christ, until he, our life, shall appear, and we too appear with him in glory.[21]

The reference to the *Parousia* is not highly developed in *SC*, but, given the concision of the theological summaries in the Liturgy Constitution, it cannot be overlooked. Jean Corbon of the *Centre des Dominicains* at Beirut, Lebanon, and the author of the section on prayer in the Catechism of the Catholic Church, produced in 1980 in French, *Liturgie de Source*, ably translated into English in 1988 as *The Wellspring of Worship*. This work can fairly be described as a sustained commentary on this eighth section of the

---

[20] *MD*, no. 165 [154].
[21] *SC*, no. 8.

Second Vatican Council's liturgical charter. Corbon's presentation of future eschatology in *Liturgie de Source* does not, as can so easily happen, set this theme over against the realised eschatology represented by *MD* and the Benedictine leaders of the Liturgical Movement. As he puts it, it is "because we are 'already' in the eternal Liturgy that its current carries us the more impatiently to its consummation."[22] In the Johannine Apocalypse, the prayer of the martyrs beneath the heavenly altar is precisely: How Long? How long before the *Parousia* comes upon us for which the Spirit and the Bride call "Come!"? This understanding perfectly reflects the understanding of *SC*. It is because the earthly Liturgy is even now the breakthrough (realised eschatology) of the heavenly that the Church is propelled toward her definitive encounter in history with the returning Lord, anticipating (future eschatology) in her worship that glorious consummation of all things.

'Chiaroscuro' complete

Let me register briefly for the sake of completeness two final points of contrast and comparison between *MD* and *SC* by asking what light is thrown on how we should evaluate the revolutionary period through which we have just passed, that question of Dickens — was it the best of times, or worst?

First, we could note with interest the way the Liturgy Constitution echoes *MD*'s warning against "undue fondness for innovation" by its insistence that interventions in the Liturgy's organic growth should only be made when imperative need of the Church commands — though in fact *SC*'s license to national liturgical commissions to propose pastoral adaptations turned out to be a blank cheque of the kind known to no bank, for this one can be perpetually re-presented![23]

Important, too, is the manner in which *MD* directly affirms the primarily latreutic character of the Liturgy, its

---

[22] Corbon, *The Wellspring of Worship*, 42.
[23] *MD*, no. 7 [7-8]; *SC*, no. 23.

theocentric nature, while *SC* makes the same point only concessively: "*Although* the Sacred Liturgy is above all things the worship of the divine Majesty, it nevertheless contains much instruction for the faithful,"[24] a nuance, possibly, but if so then, evidently, an infectious one. The Liturgy Constitution looked to liturgical reform as a means to create a better instructed laity— not at all an ignoble objective, but, in the light of *MD*, an example of using the wrong tool. In *MD*, too, the purpose of the Sacred Liturgy is to form in us that mind which was in Christ Jesus. But, as Pius explains, what this means in the context of worship is above all those attitudes with which our Great High Priest went to the offering of his saving sacrifice to the heavenly Father, insofar as redeemed creatures who are not and never will be the Redeemer, can make those movements in the Heart of Christ their own.

Conclusion

So, *was* it, then, the worst of times, rather than the best? As I suggested, the Great Revolution of the West is not the weakest analogy we can take for the effects—like those of the subsequent revolution, in large part unintended—of the Second Vatican Council. Dickens, in the thoughts he suggested for Sydney Carton on his way to the guillotine, recommended one kind of answer. That answer is not a calculation of "pros" and "cons" which, in the nature of things, our limited grasp of the ways of divine Providence makes us ill-equipped to make. Nor would so nice an answer stir in us the spiritual reconversion that response to the Lord of history always requires.

What Dickens would elicit from his readers is a hope for the future based on a readiness to learn the hard lessons both of the present and of the past. The deficiencies of one age are never entirely self-bred; they come with a genealogy. "I see," so Dickens allowed Carton to prophesy, "a beautiful city and a brilliant people rising from this abyss, and, in their struggles to be

---

[24] *SC*, no. 33; see especially *MD* nos. 75-79 [71-75], but also *passim*.

truly free in their triumphs and defeats, through long, long years to come, I see the evil of this time and of the previous time of which this is the natural birth, gradually making expiation for itself and wearing out."[25]

If it is true, as John Henry Newman claimed, that the Church constantly dies and rises again through history in imitation of her Master and Lord, how could that "slumber" and "restoration" of which the *Essay on the Development of Christian Doctrine* speaks not have its counterpart in matters of the Liturgy of the Church?[26] The renaissance to which we look forward will include, I venture to suggest, the recovery of the liturgical objectivity married with devotionalism of *MD* but also *SC*'s looking beyond the Church here and now to the final Church arrayed in the glorious garments of the redeemed when Christ comes with all his saints.

Today there are not lacking commentators who — observing the present difficulties of Roman Catholicism and its steady retreat in societies where its worship once formed the framework for living — take up the role in Dickens' novel of the knitting women: ghoulish attendants at a death scene as the "crashing engine," the guillotine, "whirrs up and falls." Those macabre assistants fail to reckon with the force of words from the Gospel according to St John which Carton cites and which underlie Newman's account of the dying and rising Church of the mysteries: "I am the Resurrection and the Life, saith the Lord, he that believeth in me, though he were dead, yet shall he live: and whosoever liveth and believeth in me, shall never die."[27]

---

[25] Dickens, *A Tale of Two Cities*, chapter three, 15.
[26] John Henry Newman, *Essay on the Development of Christian Doctrine: The Edition of 1845* (Harmondsworth: Penguin, 1974), 448.
[27] Jn 11:25-26.

MEDIATOR DEI

ENCYCLICAL OF POPE PIUS XII
ON THE SACRED LITURGY
TO THE VENERABLE BRETHREN,
THE PATRIARCHS, PRIMATES,
ARCHBISHOPS, BISHOPS,
AND OTHER ORDINARIES
IN PEACE AND COMMUNION
WITH THE APOSTOLIC SEE

Venerable Brethren,
Health and Apostolic Benediction.

INTRODUCTION

1. Mediator between God and men[1] and High Priest who has gone before us into heaven, Jesus the Son of God[2] quite clearly had one aim in view when He undertook the mission of mercy which was to endow mankind with the rich blessings of supernatural grace. Sin had disturbed the right relationship between man and his Creator; the Son of God would restore it. The children of Adam were wretched heirs to the infection of original sin; He would bring them back to their Heavenly Father, the primal source and final destiny of all things. For this reason He was not content, while He dwelt with us on earth, merely to give notice that redemption had begun, and to proclaim the long-awaited Kingdom of God, but gave Himself besides in prayer and sacrifice to the task of saving souls, even to the point of offering Himself, as He hung from the cross, a Victim unspotted unto God, to purify our conscience of dead works, to serve the living

---

[1] 1 Tim. 2:5.
[2] Cf. Heb. 4:14.

God.[3] Thus happily were all men summoned back from the byways leading them down to ruin and disaster, to be set squarely once again upon the path that leads to God. Thanks to the shedding of the blood of the Immaculate Lamb, now each might set about the personal task of achieving his own sanctification, so rendering to God the glory due to Him.

2. But what is more, the divine Redeemer has so willed it that the priestly life begun with the supplication and sacrifice of His mortal body should continue without intermission down the ages in His Mystical Body which is the Church. That is why He established a visible priesthood to offer everywhere the clean oblation[4] which would enable men from East to West, freed from the shackles of sin, to offer God that unconstrained and voluntary homage which their conscience dictates.

3. In obedience, therefore, to her Founder's behest, the Church prolongs the priestly mission of Jesus Christ mainly by means of the Sacred Liturgy. She does this in the first place at the altar, where constantly the sacrifice of the cross is represented[5] and with a single difference in the manner of its offering, renewed.[6] She does it next by means of the sacraments, those special channels through which men are made partakers in the supernatural life. She does it, finally, by offering to God, all Good and Great, the daily tribute of her prayer of praise. "What a spectacle for heaven and earth," observes Our predecessor of happy memory, Pius XI, "is not the Church at prayer! For centuries without interruption, from midnight to midnight, the divine psalmody of the inspired canticles is repeated on earth; there is no hour of the day that is not hallowed by its special liturgy; there is no state of human life that has not its part in the thanksgiving, praise, supplication and reparation of this common prayer of the Mystical Body of Christ which is His Church!"[7]

---

[3] Cf. Heb. 9:14.
[4] Cf. Mal.1:11.
[5] Cf. Council of Trent Sess. 22, c. 1.
[6] Cf. ibid., c. 2.
[7] Encyclical Letter *Caritate Christi*, May 3, 1932.

4. You are of course familiar with the fact, Venerable Brethren, that a remarkably widespread revival of scholarly interest in the Sacred Liturgy took place towards the end of the last century and has continued through the early years of this one. The movement owed its rise to commendable private initiative and more particularly to the zealous and persistent labour of several monasteries within the distinguished Order of Saint Benedict. Thus there developed in this field among many European nations, and in lands beyond the seas as well, a rivalry as welcome as it was productive of results. Indeed, the salutary fruits of this rivalry among the scholars were plain for all to see, both in the sphere of the sacred sciences, where the liturgical rites of the Western and Eastern Church were made the object of extensive research and profound study, and in the spiritual life of considerable numbers of individual Christians.

5. The majestic ceremonies of the sacrifice of the altar became better known, understood and appreciated. With more widespread and more frequent reception of the sacraments, with the beauty of the liturgical prayers more fully savoured, the worship of the Eucharist came to be regarded for what it really is: the fountain-head of genuine Christian devotion. Bolder relief was given likewise to the fact that all the faithful make up a single and very compact body with Christ for its Head, and that the Christian community is in duty bound to participate in the liturgical rites according to their station.

6. You are surely well aware that this Apostolic See has always made careful provision for the schooling of the people committed to its charge in the correct spirit and practice of the liturgy; and that it has been no less careful to insist that the sacred rites should be performed with due external dignity. In this connection We ourselves, in the course of Our traditional address to the Lenten preachers of this gracious city of Rome in 1943, urged them warmly to exhort their respective hearers to more faithful participation in the eucharistic sacrifice. Only a short while previously, with the design of rendering the prayers of the liturgy more correctly understood and their truth and unction more easy

to perceive, We arranged to have the Book of Psalms, which forms such an important part of these prayers in the Catholic Church, translated again into Latin from their original text.[8]

7. But while We derive no little satisfaction from the wholesome results of the movement just described, duty obliges Us to give serious attention to this "revival" as it is advocated in some quarters, and to take proper steps to preserve it at the outset from excess or outright perversion.

8. Indeed, though We are sorely grieved to note, on the one hand, that there are places where the spirit, understanding or practice of the Sacred Liturgy is defective, or all but inexistent, We observe with considerable anxiety and some misgiving, that elsewhere certain enthusiasts, over-eager in their search for novelty, are straying beyond the path of sound doctrine and prudence. Not seldom, in fact, they interlard their plans and hopes for a revival of the Sacred Liturgy with principles which compromise this holiest of causes in theory or practice, and sometimes even taint it with errors touching Catholic faith and ascetical doctrine.

9. Yet the integrity of faith and morals ought to be the special criterion of this sacred science, which must conform exactly to what the Church out of the abundance of her wisdom teaches and prescribes. It is, consequently, Our prerogative to commend and approve whatever is done properly, and to check or censure any aberration from the path of truth and rectitude.

10. Let not the apathetic or half-hearted imagine, however, that We agree with them when We reprove the erring and restrain the overbold. No more must the imprudent think that we are commending them when We correct the faults of those who are negligent and sluggish.

11. If in this encyclical letter We treat chiefly of the Latin liturgy, it is not because We esteem less highly the venerable liturgies of

---

[8] Cf. Apostolic Letter (Motu Proprio) *In cotidianis precibus*, March 24, 1945.

the Eastern Church, whose ancient and honourable ritual traditions are just as dear to Us. The reason lies rather in a special situation prevailing in the Western Church, of sufficient importance, it would seem, to require this exercise of Our authority.

12. With docile hearts, then, let all Christians hearken to the voice of their Common Father, who would have them, each and every one, intimately united with him as they approach the altar of God, professing the same faith, obedient to the same law, sharing in the same Sacrifice with a single intention and one sole desire. This is a duty imposed, of course, by the honour due to God. But the needs of our day and age demand it as well. After a long and cruel war which has rent whole peoples asunder with its rivalry and slaughter, men of good will are spending themselves in the effort to find the best possible way to restore peace to the world. It is, notwithstanding, Our belief that no plan or initiative can offer better prospect of success than that fervent religious spirit and zeal by which Christians must be formed and guided; in this way their common and whole-hearted acceptance of the same truth, along with their united obedience and loyalty to their appointed pastors, while rendering to God the worship due to Him, makes of them one brotherhood: "for we, being many, are one body: all that partake of one bread."[9]

---

[9] 1 Cor. 10:17.

PART I
THE NATURE, ORIGIN AND DEVELOPMENT
OF THE LITURGY

I. The Liturgy is Public Worship

13. It is unquestionably the fundamental duty of man to orientate his person and his life towards God. "For He it is to whom we must first be bound, as to an unfailing principle; to whom even our free choice must be directed as to an ultimate objective. It is He, too, whom we lose when carelessly we sin. It is He whom we must recover by our faith and trust."[10] But man turns properly to God when he acknowledges His Supreme majesty and supreme authority; when he accepts divinely revealed truths with a submissive mind; when he scrupulously obeys divine law, centring in God his every act and aspiration; when he accords, in short, due worship to the One True God by practising the virtue of religion.

14. This duty is incumbent, first of all, on men as individuals. But it also binds the whole community of human beings, grouped together by mutual social ties: mankind, too, depends on the sovereign authority of God.

15. It should be noted, moreover, that men are bound by this obligation in a special way in virtue of the fact that God has raised them to the supernatural order.

16. Thus We observe that when God institutes the Old Law, He makes provision besides for sacred rites, and determines in exact detail the rules to be observed by His people in rendering Him the worship He ordains. To this end He established various kinds of sacrifice and designated the ceremonies with which they were to be offered to Him. His enactments on all matters relating to the Ark of the Covenant, the Temple and the holy days are minute and clear. He established a sacerdotal tribe with its high priest, selected and described the vestments with which the sacred

---

[10] Saint Thomas, *Summa Theologica*, II^a II^{a3} q. 81, art. 1.

ministers were to be clothed, and every function in any way pertaining to divine worship.[11] Yet this was nothing more than a faint foreshadowing[12] of the worship which the High Priest of the New Testament was to render to the Father in heaven.

17. No sooner, in fact, "is the Word made flesh"[13] than he shows Himself to the world vested with a priestly office, making to the Eternal Father an act of submission which will continue uninterruptedly as long as He lives: "When He cometh into the world he saith...'behold I come...to do Thy Will."[14] This act He was to consummate admirably in the bloody Sacrifice of the Cross: "It is in this will we are sanctified by the oblation of the Body of Jesus Christ once."[15] He plans His active life among men with no other purpose in view. As a child He is presented to the Lord in the Temple. To the Temple He returns as a grown boy, and often afterwards to instruct the people and to pray. He fasts for forty days before beginning His public ministry. His counsel and example summon all to prayer, daily and at night as well. As Teacher of the truth He "enlighteneth every man"[16] to the end that mortals may duly acknowledge the immortal God, "not withdrawing unto perdition, but faithful to the saving of the soul."[17] As Shepherd He watches over His flock, leads it to life-giving pasture, lays down a law that none shall wander from His side, off the straight path He has pointed out, and that all shall lead holy lives imbued with His spirit and moved by His active aid. At the Last Supper He celebrates a new Pasch with solemn rite and ceremonial, and provides for its continuance through the divine institution of the Eucharist. On the morrow, lifted up between heaven and earth, He offers the saving sacrifice of His life, and pours forth, as it were, from His pierced Heart the sacraments destined to impart the treasures of redemption to the

---

[11] Cf. Book of Leviticus.
[12] Cf. Heb.10:1.
[13] John, 1:14.
[14] Heb.10:5-7.
[15] Ibid. 10:10.
[16] John, 1:9.
[17] Heb.10:39.

souls of men. All this He does with but a single aim: the glory of His Father and man's ever greater sanctification.

18. But it is His will, besides, that the worship He instituted and practised during His life on earth shall continue ever afterwards without intermission. For he has not left mankind an orphan. He still offers us the support of His powerful, unfailing intercession, acting as our "advocate with the Father."[18] He aids us likewise through His Church, where He is present indefectibly as the ages run their course: through the Church which He constituted "the pillar of truth"[19] and dispenser of grace, and which by His sacrifice on the cross, He founded, consecrated and confirmed forever.[20]

19. The Church has, therefore, in common with the Word Incarnate the aim, the obligation and the function of teaching all men the truth, of governing and directing them aright, of offering to God the pleasing and acceptable sacrifice; in this way the Church re-establishes between the Creator and His creatures that unity and harmony to which the Apostle of the Gentiles alludes in these words: "Now, therefore, you are no more strangers and foreigners; but you are fellow citizens with the saints and domestics of God, built upon the foundation of the apostles and prophets, Jesus Christ Himself being the chief corner-stone; in whom all the building, being framed together, groweth up into a holy temple in the Lord, in whom you also are built together in a habitation of God in the Spirit."[21] Thus the society founded by the divine Redeemer, whether in her doctrine and government, or in the sacrifice and sacraments instituted by Him, or finally, in the ministry, which He has confided to her charge with the outpouring of His prayer and the shedding of His blood, has no other goal or purpose than to increase ever in strength and unity.

---

[18] Cf. 1 John, 2:1.
[19] Cf. 1 Tim. 3:15.
[20] Cf. Boniface IX, *Ab origine mundi*, October 7, 1391; Callistus III, *Summus Pontifex*, January 1, 1456; Pius II, *Triumphans Pastor*, April 22, 1459; Innocent XI, *Triumphans Pastor*, October 3, 1678.
[21] Eph. 2:19-22.

20. This result is, in fact, achieved when Christ lives and thrives, as it were, in the hearts of men, and when men's hearts in turn are fashioned and expanded as though by Christ. This makes it possible for the sacred temple, where the Divine Majesty receives the acceptable worship which His law prescribes, to increase and prosper day by day in this land of exile of earth. Along with the Church, therefore, her Divine Founder is present at every liturgical function: Christ is present at the august sacrifice of the altar both in the person of His minister and above all under the eucharistic species. He is present in the sacraments, infusing into them the power which makes them ready instruments of sanctification. He is present, finally, in prayer of praise and petition we direct to God, as it is written: "Where there are two or three gathered together in My Name, there am I in the midst of them."[22] The Sacred Liturgy is, consequently, the public worship which our Redeemer as Head of the Church renders to the Father, as well as the worship which the community of the faithful renders to its Founder, and through Him to the Heavenly Father. It is, in short, the worship rendered by the Mystical Body of Christ in the entirety of its Head and members.

21. Liturgical practice begins with the very founding of the Church. The first Christians, in fact, "were persevering in the doctrine of the apostles and in the communication of the breaking of bread and in prayers."[23] Whenever their pastors can summon a little group of the faithful together, they set up an altar on which they proceed to offer the sacrifice, and around which are ranged all the other rites appropriate for the saving of souls and for the honour due to God. Among these latter rites, the first place is reserved for the sacraments, namely, the seven principal founts of salvation. There follows the celebration of the divine praises in which the faithful also join, obeying the behest of the Apostle Paul, "In all wisdom, teaching and admonishing one another in psalms, hymns and spiritual canticles, singing in grace in your

---

[22] Matt. 18:20.
[23] Acts, 2:42.

hearts to God."[24] Next comes the reading of the Law, the prophets, the gospel and the apostolic epistles; and last of all the homily or sermon in which the official head of the congregation recalls and explains the practical bearing of the commandments of the divine Master and the chief events of His life, combining instruction with appropriate exhortation and illustration for the benefit of all his listeners.

22. As circumstances and the needs of Christians warrant, public worship is organised, developed and enriched by new rites, ceremonies and regulations, always with the single end in view, "that we may use these external signs to keep us alert, learn from them what distance we have come along the road, and by them be heartened to go on further with more eager step; for the effect will be more precious the warmer the affection which precedes it."[25] Here then is a better and more suitable way to raise the heart to God. Thenceforth the priesthood of Jesus Christ is a living and continuous reality through all the ages to the end of time, since the liturgy is nothing more nor less than the exercise of this priestly function. Like her divine Head, the Church is forever present in the midst of her children. She aids and exhorts them to holiness, so that they may one day return to the Father in heaven clothed in that beauteous raiment of the supernatural. To all who are born to life on earth she gives a second, supernatural kind of birth. She arms them with the Holy Spirit for the struggle against the implacable enemy. She gathers all Christians about her altars, inviting and urging them repeatedly to take part in the celebration of the Mass, feeding them with the Bread of angels to make them ever stronger. She purifies and consoles the hearts that sin has wounded and soiled. Solemnly she consecrates those whom God has called to the priestly ministry. She fortifies with new gifts of grace the chaste nuptials of those who are destined to found and bring up a Christian family. When at last she has soothed and refreshed the closing hours of this earthly life by holy Viaticum and extreme unction, with the utmost affection she accompanies the mortal remains of her children to the grave, lays

---

[24] Col. 3:16.
[25] Saint Augustine, *Epist. 130, ad Probam*, 18.

them reverently to rest, and confides them to the protection of the cross, against the day when they will triumph over death and rise again. She has a further solemn blessing and invocation for those of her children who dedicate themselves to the service of God in the life of religious perfection. Finally, she extends to the souls in purgatory, who implore her intercession and her prayers, the helping hand which may lead them happily at last to eternal blessedness in heaven.

II. The Liturgy is Exterior and Interior Worship

23. The worship rendered by the Church to God must be, in its entirety, interior as well as exterior. It is exterior because the nature of man as a composite of body and soul requires it to be so. Likewise, because divine Providence has disposed that "while we recognise God visibly, we may be drawn by Him to love of things unseen."[26] Every impulse of the human heart, besides, expresses itself naturally through the senses; and the worship of God, being the concern not merely of individuals but of the whole community of mankind, must therefore be social as well. This obviously it cannot be unless religious activity is also organised and manifested outwardly. Exterior worship, finally, reveals and emphasises the unity of the mystical Body, feeds new fuel to its holy zeal, fortifies its energy, intensifies its action day by day: "for although the ceremonies themselves can claim no perfection or sanctity in their own right, they are, nevertheless, the outward acts of religion, designed to rouse the heart, like signals of a sort, to veneration of the sacred realities, and to raise the mind to meditation on the supernatural. They serve to foster piety, to kindle the flame of charity, to increase our faith and deepen our devotion. They provide instruction for simple folk, decoration for divine worship, continuity of religious practice. They make it possible to tell genuine Christians from their false or heretical counterparts."[27]

---

[26] *Missale Romanum*, Preface for Christmas.
[27] Giovanni Cardinal Bona, *De divina psalmodia*, c. 19, par. 3, 1.

24. But the chief element of divine worship must be interior. For we must always live in Christ and give ourselves to Him completely, so that in Him, with Him and through Him the Heavenly Father may be duly glorified. The Sacred Liturgy requires, however, that both of these elements be intimately linked with each other. This recommendation the liturgy itself is careful to repeat, as often as it prescribes an exterior act of worship. Thus we are urged, when there is question of fasting, for example, "to give interior effect to our outward observance."[28] Otherwise religion clearly amounts to mere formalism, without meaning and without content. You recall, Venerable Brethren, how the divine Master expels from the sacred temple, as unworthy to worship there, people who pretend to honour God with nothing but neat and well turned phrases, like actors in a theatre, and think themselves perfectly capable of working out their eternal salvation without plucking their inveterate vices from their hearts.[29] It is, therefore, the keen desire of the Church that all of the faithful kneel at the feet of the Redeemer to tell Him how much they venerate and love Him. She wants them present in crowds - like the children whose joyous cries accompanied His entry into Jerusalem - to sing their hymns and chant their song of praise and thanksgiving to Him who is King of Kings and Source of every blessing. She would have them move their lips in prayer, sometimes in petition, sometimes in joy and gratitude, and in this way experience His merciful aid and power like the apostles at the lakeside of Tiberias, or abandon themselves totally, like Peter on Mount Tabor, to mystic union with the eternal God in contemplation.

25. It is an error, consequently, and a mistake to think of the Sacred Liturgy as merely the outward or visible part of divine worship or as an ornamental ceremonial. No less erroneous is the notion that it consists solely in a list of laws and prescriptions according to which the ecclesiastical hierarchy orders the sacred rites to be performed.

---

[28] *Missale Romanum,* Secret for Thursday after the Second Sunday of Lent.
[29] Cf. Mark, 7:6 and Isaias, 29:13.

26. It should be clear to all, then, that God cannot be honoured worthily unless the mind and heart turn to Him in quest of the perfect life, and that the worship rendered to God by the Church in union with her divine Head is the most efficacious means of achieving sanctity.

27. This efficacy, where there is question of the eucharistic sacrifice and the sacraments, derives first of all and principally from the act itself (*ex opere operato*). But if one considers the part which the Immaculate Spouse of Jesus Christ takes in the action, embellishing the sacrifice and sacraments with prayer and sacred ceremonies, or if one refers to the "sacramentals" and the other rites instituted by the hierarchy of the Church, then its effectiveness is due rather to the action of the Church (*ex opere operantis Ecclesiæ*), inasmuch as she is holy and acts always in closest union with her Head.

28. In this connection, Venerable Brethren, We desire to direct your attention to certain recent theories touching a so-called "objective" piety. While these theories attempt, it is true, to throw light on the mystery of the Mystical Body, on the effective reality of sanctifying grace, on the action of God in the sacraments and in the Mass, it is nonetheless apparent that they tend to belittle, or pass over in silence, what they call "subjective," or "personal" piety.

29. It is an unquestionable fact that the work of our redemption is continued, and that its fruits are imparted to us, during the celebration of the liturgy, notably in the august sacrifice of the altar. Christ acts each day to save us, in the sacraments and in His holy sacrifice. By means of them He is constantly atoning for the sins of mankind, constantly consecrating it to God. Sacraments and sacrifice do, then, possess that "objective" power to make us really and personally sharers in the divine life of Jesus Christ. Not from any ability of our own, but by the power of God, are they endowed with the capacity to unite the piety of members with that of the Head, and to make this, in a sense, the action of the whole community. From these profound considerations some are led to conclude that all Christian piety must be centred in the

mystery of the Mystical Body of Christ, with no regard for what is "personal" or "subjective, as they would have it. As a result they feel that all other religious exercises not directly connected with the Sacred Liturgy, and performed outside public worship should be omitted.

30. But though the principles set forth above are excellent, it must be plain to everyone that the conclusions drawn from them respecting two sorts of piety are false, insidious and quite pernicious.

31. Very truly, the sacraments and the sacrifice of the altar, being Christ's own actions, must be held to be capable in themselves of conveying and dispensing grace from the divine Head to the members of the Mystical Body. But if they are to produce their proper effect, it is absolutely necessary that our hearts be properly disposed to receive them. Hence the warning of Paul the Apostle with reference to holy communion, "But let a man first prove himself; and then let him eat of this bread and drink of the chalice."[30] This explains why the Church in a brief and significant phrase calls the various acts of mortification, especially those practised during the season of Lent, "the Christian army's defences."[31] They represent, in fact, the personal effort and activity of members who desire, as grace urges and aids them, to join forces with their Captain - "that we may discover...in our Captain," to borrow St Augustine's words, "the fountain of grace itself."[32] But observe that these members are alive, endowed and equipped with an intelligence and will of their own. It follows that they are strictly required to put their own lips to the fountain, imbibe and absorb for themselves the life-giving water, and rid themselves personally of anything that might hinder its nutritive effect in their souls. Emphatically, therefore, the work of redemption, which in itself is independent of our will, requires a serious interior effort on our part if we are to achieve eternal salvation.

---

[30] 1 Cor.11:28.
[31] *Missale Romanum,* Ash Wednesday; Prayer after the imposition of ashes.
[32] *De praedestinatione sanctorum,* 31.

32. If the private and interior devotion of individuals were to neglect the august sacrifice of the altar and the sacraments, and to withdraw them from the stream of vital energy that flows from Head to members, it would indeed be sterile, and deserve to be condemned. But when devotional exercises, and pious practices in general, not strictly connected with the Sacred Liturgy, confine themselves to merely human acts, with the express purpose of directing these latter to the Father in heaven, of rousing people to repentance and holy fear of God, of weaning them from the seductions of the world and its vice, and leading them back to the difficult path of perfection, then certainly such practices are not only highly praiseworthy but absolutely indispensable, because they expose the dangers threatening the spiritual life; because they promote the acquisition of virtue; and because they increase the fervour and generosity with which we are bound to dedicate all that we are and all that we have to the service of Jesus Christ. Genuine and real piety, which the Angelic Doctor calls "devotion," and which is the principal act of the virtue of religion - that act which correctly relates and fitly directs men to God; and by which they freely and spontaneously give themselves to the worship of God in its fullest sense[33] - piety of this authentic sort needs meditation on the supernatural realities and spiritual exercises, if it is to be nurtured, stimulated and sustained, and if it is to prompt us to lead a more perfect life. For the Christian religion, practised as it should be, demands that the will especially be consecrated to God and exert its influence on all the other spiritual faculties. But every act of the will presupposes an act of the intelligence, and before one can express the desire and the intention of offering oneself in sacrifice to the eternal Godhead, a knowledge of the facts and truths which make religion a duty is altogether necessary. One must first know, for instance, man's last end and the supremacy of the Divine Majesty; after that, our common duty of submission to our Creator; and, finally, the inexhaustible treasures of love with which God yearns to enrich us, as well as the necessity of supernatural grace for the achievement of our destiny, and that

---

[33] Cf. Saint Thomas, *Summa Theologica*, II^a II^{a3}, q. 82, art. 1.

special path marked out for us by divine Providence in virtue of the fact that we have been united, one and all, like members of a body, to Jesus Christ the Head. But further, since our hearts, disturbed as they are at times by the lower appetites, do not always respond to motives of love, it is also extremely helpful to let consideration and contemplation of the justice of God provoke us on occasion to salutary fear, and guide us thence to Christian humility, repentance and amendment.

33. But it will not do to possess these facts and truths after the fashion of an abstract memory lesson or lifeless commentary. They must lead to practical results. They must impel us to subject our senses and their faculties to reason, as illuminated by the Catholic faith. They must help to cleanse and purify the heart, uniting it to Christ more intimately every day, growing ever more to His likeness, and drawing from Him the divine inspiration and strength of which it stands in need. They must serve as increasingly effective incentives to action: urging men to produce good fruit, to perform their individual duties faithfully, to give themselves eagerly to the regular practice of their religion and the energetic exercise of virtue. "You are Christ's, and Christ is God's."[34] Let everything, therefore, have its proper place and arrangement; let everything be "theocentric," so to speak, if we really wish to direct everything to the glory of God through the life and power which flow from the divine Head into our hearts: "Having therefore, brethren, a confidence in the entering into the holies by the blood of Christ, a new and living way which He both dedicated for us through the veil, that is to say, His flesh, and a high priest over the house of God; let us draw near with a true heart, in fullness of faith, having our hearts sprinkled clean from an evil conscience and our bodies washed with pure water, let us hold fast the confession of our hope without wavering...and let us consider one another, to provoke unto charity and to good works."[35]

---

[34] Cf. 1 Cor. 3:23.
[35] Heb. 10:19-24.

34. Here is the source of the harmony and equilibrium which prevails among the members of the Mystical Body of Jesus Christ. When the Church teaches us our Catholic faith and exhorts us to obey the commandments of Christ, she is paving a way for her priestly, sanctifying action in its highest sense; she disposes us likewise for more serious meditation on the life of the divine Redeemer and guides us to profounder knowledge of the mysteries of faith where we may draw the supernatural sustenance, strength and vitality that enable us to progress safely, through Christ, towards a more perfect life. Not only through her ministers but with the help of the faithful individually, who have imbibed in this fashion the spirit of Christ, the Church endeavours to permeate with this same spirit the life and labours of men - their private and family life, their social, even economic and political life - that all who are called God's children may reach more readily the end He has proposed for them.

35. Such action on the part of individual Christians, then, along with the ascetic effort promoting them to purify their hearts, actually stimulates in the faithful those energies which enable them to participate in the august sacrifice of the altar with better dispositions. They now can receive the sacraments with more abundant fruit, and come from the celebration of the sacred rites more eager, more firmly resolved to pray and deny themselves like Christians, to answer the inspirations and invitation of divine grace and to imitate daily more closely the virtues of our Redeemer. And all of this not simply for their own advantage, but for that of the whole Church, where whatever good is accomplished proceeds from the power of her Head and redounds to the advancement of all her members.

36. In the spiritual life, consequently, there can be no opposition between the action of God, who pours forth His grace into men's hearts so that the work of the redemption may always abide, and the tireless collaboration of man, who must not render vain the gift of God.[36] No more can the efficacy of the external administration of the sacraments, which comes from the rite itself

---

[36] Cf. 2 Cor. 6:1.

(*ex opere operato*), be opposed to the meritorious action of their ministers or recipients, which we call the agent's action (*opus operantis*). Similarly, no conflict exists between public prayer and prayers in private, between morality and contemplation, between the ascetical life and devotion to the liturgy. Finally, there is no opposition between the jurisdiction and teaching office of the ecclesiastical hierarchy, and the specifically priestly power exercised in the sacred ministry.

37. Considering their special designation to perform the liturgical functions of the holy sacrifice and Divine Office, the Church has serious reason for prescribing that the ministers she assigns to the service of the sanctuary and members of religious institutes betake themselves at stated times to mental prayer, to examination of conscience, and to various other spiritual exercises.[37] Unquestionably, liturgical prayer, being the public supplication of the illustrious Spouse of Jesus Christ, is superior in excellence to private prayers. But this superior worth does not at all imply contrast or incompatibility between these two kinds of prayer. For both merge harmoniously in the single spirit which animates them, "Christ is all and in all."[38] Both tend to the same objective: until Christ be formed in us.[39]

III. The Liturgy is under the Hierarchy of the Church

38. For a better and more accurate understanding of the Sacred Liturgy another of its characteristic features, no less important, needs to be considered.

39. The Church is a society, and as such requires an authority and hierarchy of her own. Though it is true that all the members of the Mystical Body partake of the same blessings and pursue the same objective, they do not all enjoy the same powers, nor are they all qualified to perform the same acts. The divine Redeemer has willed, as a matter of fact, that His Kingdom should be built

---

[37] Cf. Code of Canon Law, can. 125, 126, 565, 571, 595, 1367.
[38] Col. 3:11.
[39] Cf. Gal. 4:19.

and solidly supported, as it were, on a holy order, which resembles in some sort the heavenly hierarchy.

40. Only to the apostles, and thenceforth to those on whom their successors have imposed hands, is granted the power of the priesthood, in virtue of which they represent the person of Jesus Christ before their people, acting at the same time as representatives of their people before God. This priesthood is not transmitted by heredity or human descent. It does not emanate from the Christian community. It is not a delegation from the people. Prior to acting as representative of the community before the throne of God, the priest is the ambassador of the divine Redeemer. He is God's vice-regent in the midst of his flock precisely because Jesus Christ is Head of that body of which Christians are the members. The power entrusted to him, therefore, bears no natural resemblance to anything human. It is entirely supernatural. It comes from God. "As the Father hath sent me, I also send you[40]...he that heareth you heareth me[41]...go ye into the whole world and preach the gospel to every creature; he that believeth and is baptised shall be saved."[42]

41. That is why the visible, external priesthood of Jesus Christ is not handed down indiscriminately to all members of the Church in general, but is conferred on designated men, through what may be called the spiritual generation of holy orders.

42. This latter, one of the seven sacraments, not only imparts the grace appropriate to the clerical function and state of life, but imparts an indelible "character" besides, indicating the sacred ministers' conformity to Jesus Christ the Priest and qualifying them to perform those official acts of religion by which men are sanctified and God is duly glorified in keeping with the divine laws and regulations.

---

[40] John, 20:21.
[41] Luke, 10:16.
[42] Mark, 16:15-16.

43. In the same way, actually, that baptism is the distinctive mark of all Christians, and serves to differentiate them from those who have not been cleansed in this purifying stream and consequently are not members of Christ, the sacrament of holy orders sets the priest apart from the rest of the faithful who have not received this consecration. For they alone, in answer to an inward supernatural call, have entered the august ministry, where they are assigned to service in the sanctuary and become, as it were, the instruments God uses to communicate supernatural life from on high to the Mystical Body of Jesus Christ. Add to this, as We have noted above, the fact that they alone have been marked with the indelible sign "conforming" them to Christ the Priest, and that their hands alone have been consecrated "in order that whatever they bless may be blessed, whatever they consecrate may become sacred and holy, in the name of our Lord Jesus Christ."[43] Let all, then, who would live in Christ flock to their priests. By them they will be supplied with the comforts and food of the spiritual life. From them they will procure the medicine of salvation assuring their cure and happy recovery from the fatal sickness of their sins. The priest, finally, will bless their homes, consecrate their families and help them, as they breathe their last, across the threshold of eternal happiness.

44. Since, therefore, it is the priest chiefly who performs the Sacred Liturgy in the name of the Church, its organisation, regulation and details cannot but be subject to Church authority. This conclusion, based on the nature of Christian worship itself, is further confirmed by the testimony of history.

45. Additional proof of this indefeasible right of the ecclesiastical hierarchy lies in the circumstances that the Sacred Liturgy is intimately bound up with doctrinal propositions which the Church proposes to be perfectly true and certain, and must as a consequence conform to the decrees respecting Catholic faith issued by the supreme teaching authority of the Church with a view to safeguarding the integrity of the religion revealed by God.

---

[43] *Pontificale Romanum,* Ordination of a priest: anointing of hands.

46. On this subject We judge it Our duty to rectify an attitude with which you are doubtless familiar, Venerable Brethren. We refer to the error and fallacious reasoning of those who have claimed that the Sacred Liturgy is a kind of proving ground for the truths to be held of faith, meaning by this that the Church is obliged to declare such a doctrine sound when it is found to have produced fruits of piety and sanctity through the sacred rites of the liturgy, and to reject it otherwise. Hence the epigram, *'Lex orandi, lex credendi"* - the law for prayer is the law for faith.

47. But this is not what the Church teaches and enjoins. The worship she offers to God, all good and great, is a continuous profession of Catholic faith and a continuous exercise of hope and charity, as Augustine puts it tersely. "God is to be worshipped," he says, "by faith, hope and charity."[44] In the Sacred Liturgy we profess the Catholic faith explicitly and openly, not only by the celebration of the mysteries, and by offering the holy sacrifice and administering the sacraments, but also by saying or singing the credo or Symbol of the faith - it is indeed the sign and badge, as it were, of the Christian - along with other texts, and likewise by the reading of holy scripture, written under the inspiration of the Holy Ghost. The entire liturgy, therefore, has the Catholic faith for its content, inasmuch as it bears public witness to the faith of the Church.

48. For this reason, whenever there was question of defining a truth revealed by God, the Sovereign Pontiff and the Councils in their recourse to the "theological sources," as they are called, have not seldom drawn many an argument from this sacred science of the liturgy. For an example in point, Our predecessor of immortal memory, Pius IX, so argued when he proclaimed the Immaculate Conception of the Virgin Mary. Similarly during the discussion of a doubtful or controversial truth, the Church and the Holy Fathers have not failed to look to the age-old and age-honoured sacred rites for enlightenment. Hence the well-known and venerable maxim, *"Legem credendi lex statuat supplicandi"* - let

---

[44] *Enchiridion*, c. 3.

the rule for prayer determine the rule of belief.[45] The Sacred Liturgy, consequently, does not decide or determine independently and of itself what is of Catholic faith. More properly, since the liturgy is also a profession of eternal truths, and subject, as such, to the supreme teaching authority of the Church, it can supply proofs and testimony, quite clearly, of no little value, towards the determination of a particular point of Christian doctrine. But if one desires to differentiate and describe the relationship between faith and the Sacred Liturgy in absolute and general terms, it is perfectly correct to say, *"Lex credendi legem statuat supplicandi"* - let the rule of belief determine the rule of prayer. The same holds true for the other theological virtues also, *"In...fide, spe, caritate continuato desiderio semper oramus"* - we pray always, with constant yearning in faith, hope and charity.[46]

IV. The Progress and the Development of the Liturgy

49. From time immemorial the ecclesiastical hierarchy has exercised this right in matters liturgical. It has organised and regulated divine worship, enriching it constantly with new splendour and beauty, to the glory of God and the spiritual profit of Christians. What is more, it has not been slow - keeping the substance of the Mass and sacraments carefully intact - to modify what it deemed not altogether fitting, and to add what appeared more likely to increase the honour paid to Jesus Christ and the august Trinity, and to instruct and stimulate the Christian people to greater advantage.[47]

50. The Sacred Liturgy does, in fact, include divine as well as human elements. The former, instituted as they have been by God, cannot be changed in any way by men. But the human components admit of various modifications, as the needs of the age, circumstance and the good of souls may require, and as the ecclesiastical hierarchy, under guidance of the Holy Spirit, may have authorised. This will explain the marvellous variety of

---

[45] *De gratia Dei* "Indiculus."

[46] Saint Augustine, *Epist. 130, ad Probam*, 18.

[47] Cf. Constitution *Divini cultus*, December 20, 1928.

Eastern and Western rites. Here is the reason for the gradual addition, through successive development, of particular religious customs and practices of piety only faintly discernible in earlier times. Hence likewise it happens from time to time that certain devotions long since forgotten are revived and practised anew. All these developments attest the abiding life of the immaculate Spouse of Jesus Christ through these many centuries. They are the sacred language she uses, as the ages run their course, to profess to her divine Spouse her own faith along with that of the nations committed to her charge, and her own unfailing love. They furnish proof, besides, of the wisdom of the teaching method she employs to arouse and nourish constantly the "Christian instinct."

51. Several causes, really have been instrumental in the progress and development of the Sacred Liturgy during the long and glorious life of the Church.

52. Thus, for example, as Catholic doctrine on the Incarnate Word of God, the eucharistic sacrament and sacrifice, and Mary the Virgin Mother of God came to be determined with greater certitude and clarity, new ritual forms were introduced through which the acts of the liturgy proceeded to reproduce this brighter light issuing from the decrees of the teaching authority of the Church, and to reflect it, in a sense so that it might reach the minds and hearts of Christ's people more readily.

53. The subsequent advances in ecclesiastical discipline for the administering of the sacraments, that of penance for example; the institution and later suppression of the catechumenate; and again, the practice of eucharistic communion under a single species, adopted in the Latin Church; these developments were assuredly responsible in no little measure for the modification of the ancient ritual in the course of time, and for the gradual introduction of new rites considered more in accord with prevailing discipline in these matters.

54. Just as notable a contribution to this progressive transformation was made by devotional trends and practices not

directly related to the Sacred Liturgy, which began to appear, by God's wonderful design, in later periods, and grew to be so popular. We may instance the spread and ever mounting ardour of devotion to the Blessed Eucharist, devotion to the most bitter passion of our Redeemer, devotion to the most Sacred Heart of Jesus, to the Virgin Mother of God and to her most chaste spouse.

55. Other manifestations of piety have also played their circumstantial part in this same liturgical development. Among them may be cited the public pilgrimages to the tombs of the martyrs prompted by motives of devotion, the special periods of fasting instituted for the same reason, and lastly, in this gracious city of Rome, the penitential recitation of the litanies during the "station" processions, in which even the Sovereign Pontiff frequently joined.

56. It is likewise easy to understand that the progress of the fine arts, those of architecture, painting and music above all, has exerted considerable influence on the choice and disposition of the various external features of the Sacred Liturgy.

57. The Church has further used her right of control over liturgical observance to protect the purity of divine worship against abuse from dangerous and imprudent innovations introduced by private individuals and particular churches. Thus it came about - during the 16th century, when usages and customs of this sort had become increasingly prevalent and exaggerated, and when private initiative in matters liturgical threatened to compromise the integrity of faith and devotion, to the great advantage of heretics and further spread of their errors - that in the year 1588, Our predecessor Sixtus V of immortal memory established the Sacred Congregation of Rites, charged with the defence of the legitimate rites of the Church and with the prohibition of any spurious innovation.[48] This body fulfils even today the official function of supervision and legislation with regard to all matters touching the Sacred Liturgy.[49]

---

[48] Constitution *Immensa*, January 22, 1588.
[49] Code of Canon Law, can. 253.

V. The Development of the Liturgy may not be left to Private Judgement

58. It follows from this that the Sovereign Pontiff alone enjoys the right to recognise and establish any practice touching the worship of God, to introduce and approve new rites, as also to modify those he judges to require modification.[50] Bishops, for their part, have the right and duty carefully to watch over the exact observance of the prescriptions of the sacred canons respecting divine worship.[51] Private individuals, therefore, even though they be clerics, may not be left to decide for themselves in these holy and venerable matters, involving as they do the religious life of Christian society along with the exercise of the priesthood of Jesus Christ and worship of God; concerned as they are with the honour due to the Blessed Trinity, the Word Incarnate and His august mother and the other saints, and with the salvation of souls as well. For the same reason no private person has any authority to regulate external practices of this kind, which are intimately bound up with Church discipline and with the order, unity and concord of the Mystical Body and frequently even with the integrity of Catholic faith itself.

59. The Church is without question a living organism, and as an organism, in respect of the Sacred Liturgy also, she grows, matures, develops, adapts and accommodates herself to temporal needs and circumstances, provided only that the integrity of her doctrine be safeguarded. This notwithstanding, the temerity and daring of those who introduce novel liturgical practices, or call for the revival of obsolete rites out of harmony with prevailing laws and rubrics, deserve severe reproof. It has pained Us grievously to note, Venerable Brethren, that such innovations are actually being introduced, not merely in minor details but in matters of major importance as well. We instance, in point of fact, those who make use of the vernacular in the celebration of the august eucharistic sacrifice; those who transfer certain feast-days

---

[50] Cf. ibid., can. 1257.
[51] Cf. ibid., can. 1261.

- which have been appointed and established after mature deliberation - to other dates; those, finally, who delete from the prayerbooks approved for public use the sacred texts of the Old Testament, deeming them little suited and inopportune for modern times.

60. The use of the Latin language, customary in a considerable portion of the Church, is a manifest and beautiful sign of unity, as well as an effective antidote for any corruption of doctrinal truth. In spite of this, the use of the mother tongue in connection with several of the rites may be of much advantage to the people. But the Apostolic See alone is empowered to grant this permission. It is forbidden, therefore, to take any action whatever of this nature without having requested and obtained such consent, since the Sacred Liturgy, as We have said, is entirely subject to the discretion and approval of the Holy See.

61. The same reasoning holds in the case of some persons who are bent on the restoration of all the ancient rites and ceremonies indiscriminately. The liturgy of the early ages is most certainly worthy of all veneration. But ancient usage must not be esteemed more suitable and proper, either in its own right or in its significance for later times and new situations, on the simple ground that it carries the savour and aroma of antiquity. The more recent liturgical rites likewise deserve reverence and respect. They, too, owe their inspiration to the Holy Spirit, who assists the Church in every age even to the consummation of the world.[52] They are equally the resources used by the majestic Spouse of Jesus Christ to promote and procure the sanctity of man.

62. Assuredly it is a wise and most laudable thing to return in spirit and affection to the sources of the Sacred Liturgy. For research in this field of study, by tracing it back to its origins, contributes valuable assistance towards a more thorough and careful investigation of the significance of feast-days, and of the meaning of the texts and sacred ceremonies employed on their

---

[52] Cf. Matt. 28:20.

occasion. But it is neither wise nor laudable to reduce everything to antiquity by every possible device. Thus, to cite some instances, one would be straying from the straight path were he to wish the altar restored to its primitive table form; were he to want black excluded as a colour for the liturgical vestments; were he to forbid the use of sacred images and statues in Churches; were he to order the crucifix so designed that the divine Redeemer's body shows no trace of His cruel sufferings; and lastly were he to disdain and reject polyphonic music or singing in parts, even where it conforms to regulations issued by the Holy See.

63. Clearly no sincere Catholic can refuse to accept the formulation of Christian doctrine more recently elaborated and proclaimed as dogmas by the Church, under the inspiration and guidance of the Holy Spirit with abundant fruit for souls, because it pleases him to hark back to the old formulas. No more can any Catholic in his right senses repudiate existing legislation of the Church to revert to prescriptions based on the earliest sources of canon law. Just as obviously unwise and mistaken is the zeal of one who in matters liturgical would go back to the rites and usage of antiquity, discarding the new patterns introduced by disposition of divine Providence to meet the changes of circumstances and situation.

64. This way of acting bids fair to revive the exaggerated and senseless antiquarianism to which the illegal Council of Pistoia gave rise. It likewise attempts to reinstate a series of errors which were responsible for the calling of that meeting as well as for those resulting from it, with grievous harm to souls, and which the Church, the ever watchful guardian of the "deposit of faith" committed to her charge by her divine Founder, had every right and reason to condemn.[53] For perverse designs and ventures of this sort tend to paralyse and weaken that process of sanctification by which the Sacred Liturgy directs the sons of adoption to their Heavenly Father of their souls' salvation.

---

[53] Cf. Pius VI, Constitution *Auctorem fidei*, August 28, 1794, nn. 31-34, 39, 62, 66, 69-74.

65. In every measure taken, then, let proper contact with the ecclesiastical hierarchy be maintained. Let no one arrogate to himself the right to make regulations and impose them on others at will. Only the Sovereign Pontiff, as the successor of Saint Peter, charged by the divine Redeemer with the feeding of His entire flock,[54] and with him, in obedience to the Apostolic See, the bishops "whom the Holy Ghost has placed . . . to rule the Church of God,"[55] have the right and the duty to govern the Christian people. Consequently, Venerable Brethren, whenever you assert your authority - even on occasion with wholesome severity - you are not merely acquitting yourselves of your duty; you are defending the very will of the Founder of the Church.

---

[54] Cf. John, 21:15-17.
[55] Acts, 20:28.

PART II
EUCHARISTIC WORSHIP

I. The Nature of the Eucharistic Sacrifice

66. The mystery of the most Holy Eucharist which Christ, the High Priest instituted, and which He commands to be continually renewed in the Church by His ministers, is the culmination and centre, as it were, of the Christian religion. We consider it opportune in speaking about the crowning act of the Sacred Liturgy, to delay for a little while and call your attention, Venerable Brethren, to this most important subject.

67. Christ the Lord, "Eternal Priest according to the order of Melchisedech,"[56] "loving His own who were of the world,"[57] "at the last supper, on the night He was betrayed, wishing to leave His beloved Spouse, the Church, a visible sacrifice such as the nature of men requires, that would re-present the bloody sacrifice offered once on the cross, and perpetuate its memory to the end of time, and whose salutary virtue might be applied in remitting those sins which we daily commit...offered His body and blood under the species of bread and wine to God the Father, and under the same species allowed the apostles, whom He at that time constituted the priests of the New Testament, to partake thereof; commanding them and their successors in the priesthood to make the same offering."[58]

68. The august sacrifice of the altar, then, is no mere empty commemoration of the passion and death of Jesus Christ, but a true and proper act of sacrifice, whereby the High Priest by an unbloody immolation offers Himself a most acceptable victim to the Eternal Father, as He did upon the cross. "It is one and the same victim; the same person now offers it by the ministry of His

---

[56] Ps.109:4.
[57] John, 13:1.
[58] Council of Trent, Sess. 22, c. 1.

priests, who then offered Himself on the cross, the manner of offering alone being different."[59]

69. The priest is the same, Jesus Christ, whose Sacred Person His minister represents. Now the minister, by reason of the sacerdotal consecration which he has received, is made like to the High Priest and possesses the power of performing actions in virtue of Christ's very person.[60] Wherefore in his priestly activity he in a certain manner "lends his tongue, and gives his hand" to Christ.[61]

70. Likewise the victim is the same, namely, our divine Redeemer in His human nature with His true body and blood. The manner, however, in which Christ is offered is different. On the cross He completely offered Himself and all His sufferings to God, and the immolation of the victim was brought about by the bloody death, which He underwent of His free will. But on the altar, by reason of the glorified state of His human nature, "death shall have no more dominion over Him,"[62] and so the shedding of His blood is impossible; still, according to the plan of divine wisdom, the sacrifice of our Redeemer is shown forth in an admirable manner by external signs which are the symbols of His death. For by the "transubstantiation" of bread into the body of Christ and of wine into His blood, His body and blood are both really present: now the eucharistic species under which He is present symbolise the actual separation of His body and blood. Thus the commemorative representation of His death, which actually took place on Calvary, is repeated in every sacrifice of the altar, seeing that Jesus Christ is symbolically shown by separate symbols to be in a state of victimhood.

71. Moreover, the appointed ends are the same. The first of these is to give glory to the Heavenly Father. From His birth to His death Jesus Christ burned with zeal for the divine glory; and the offering of His blood upon the cross rose to heaven in an odour of

---

[59] Ibid., c. 2.
[60] Cf. Saint Thomas, *Summa Theologica*, III^a, q. 22, art. 4.
[61] Saint John Chrysostom, *In Joann. Hom.*, 86:4.
[62] Rom. 6:9.

sweetness. To perpetuate this praise, the members of the Mystical Body are united with their divine Head in the eucharistic sacrifice, and with Him, together with the Angels and Archangels, they sing immortal praise to God[63] and give all honour and glory to the Father Almighty.[64]

72. The second end is duly to give thanks to God. Only the divine Redeemer, as the eternal Father's most beloved Son whose immense love He knew, could offer Him a worthy return of gratitude. This was His intention and desire at the Last Supper when He "gave thanks."[65] He did not cease to do so when hanging upon the cross, nor does He fail to do so in the august sacrifice of the altar, which is an act of thanksgiving or a "eucharistic" act; since this "is truly meet and just, right and availing unto salvation."[66]

73. The third end proposed is that of expiation, propitiation and reconciliation. Certainly, no one was better fitted to make satisfaction to Almighty God for all the sins of men than was Christ. Therefore, He desired to be immolated upon the cross "as a propitiation for our sins, not for ours only but also for those of the whole world"[67] and likewise He daily offers Himself upon our altars for our redemption, that we may be rescued from eternal damnation and admitted into the company of the elect. This He does, not for us only who are in this mortal life, but also "for all who rest in Christ, who have gone before us with the sign of faith and repose in the sleep of peace;"[68] for whether we live, or whether we die "still we are not separated from the one and only Christ."[69]

74. The fourth end, finally, is that of impetration. Man, being the prodigal son, has made bad use of and dissipated the goods

---

[63] Cf. *Missale Romanum*, Preface.
[64] Cf. ibid., Canon.
[65] Mark, 14:23.
[66] *Missale Romanum*, Preface.
[67] 1 John, 2:2.
[68] *Missale Romanum*, Canon of the Mass.
[69] Saint Augustine, *De Trinit.*, Book XIII, c. 19.

which he received from his Heavenly Father. Accordingly, he has been reduced to the utmost poverty and to extreme degradation. However, Christ on the cross "offering prayers and supplications with a loud cry and tears, has been heard for His reverence."[70] Likewise upon the altar He is our mediator with God in the same efficacious manner, so that we may be filled with every blessing and grace.

75. It is easy, therefore, to understand why the holy Council of Trent lays down that by means of the eucharistic sacrifice the saving virtue of the cross is imparted to us for the remission of the sins we daily commit.[71]

76. Now the Apostle of the Gentiles proclaims the copious plenitude and the perfection of the sacrifice of the cross, when he says that Christ by one oblation has perfected for ever them that are sanctified.[72] For the merits of this sacrifice, since they are altogether boundless and immeasurable, know no limits; for they are meant for all men of every time and place. This follows from the fact that in this sacrifice the God-Man is the priest and victim; that His immolation was entirely perfect, as was His obedience to the will of His eternal Father; and also that He suffered death as the Head of the human race: "See how we were bought: Christ hangs upon the cross, see at what a price He makes His purchase . . . He sheds His blood, He buys with His blood, He buys with the blood of the Spotless Lamb, He buys with the blood of God's only Son. He who buys is Christ; the price is His blood; the possession bought is the world."[73]

77. This purchase, however, does not immediately have its full effect; since Christ, after redeeming the world at the lavish cost of His own blood, still must come into complete possession of the souls of men. Wherefore, that the redemption and salvation of each person and of future generations unto the end of time may

---

[70] Heb. 5:7.

[71] Cf. Sess. 22, c. 1.

[72] Cf. Heb. 10:14.

[73] Saint Augustine, *Enarr. in Ps.* 147, n. 16.

be effectively accomplished, and be acceptable to God, it is necessary that men should individually come into vital contact with the sacrifice of the cross, so that the merits, which flow from it, should be imparted to them. In a certain sense it can be said that on Calvary Christ built a font of purification and salvation which He filled with the blood He shed; but if men do not bathe in it and there wash away the stains of their iniquities, they can never be purified and saved.

78. The co-operation of the faithful is required so that sinners may be individually purified in the blood of the Lamb. For though, speaking generally, Christ reconciled by His painful death the whole human race with the Father, He wished that all should approach and be drawn to His cross, especially by means of the sacraments and the eucharistic sacrifice, to obtain the salutary fruits produced by Him upon it. Through this active and individual participation, the members of the Mystical Body not only become daily more like to their divine Head, but the life flowing from the Head is imparted to the members, so that we can each repeat the words of St Paul, "With Christ I am nailed to the cross: I live, now not I, but Christ liveth in me."[74] We have already explained sufficiently and of set purpose on another occasion, that Jesus Christ "when dying on the cross, bestowed upon His Church, as a completely gratuitous gift, the immense treasure of the redemption. But when it is a question of distributing this treasure, He not only commits the work of sanctification to His Immaculate Spouse, but also wishes that, to a certain extent, sanctity should derive from her activity."[75]

79. The august sacrifice of the altar is, as it were, the supreme instrument whereby the merits won by the divine Redeemer upon the cross are distributed to the faithful: "as often as this commemorative sacrifice is offered, there is wrought the work of our Redemption."[76] This, however, so far from lessening the dignity of the actual sacrifice on Calvary, rather proclaims and

---

[74] Gal. 2:19-20.
[75] Encyclical Letter, *Mystici Corporis*, June 29, 1943.
[76] Roman Missal, Secret of the Ninth Sunday after Pentecost.

renders more manifest its greatness and its necessity, as the Council of Trent declares.[77] Its daily immolation reminds us that there is no salvation except in the cross of our Lord Jesus Christ[78] and that God Himself wishes that there should be a continuation of this sacrifice "from the rising of the sun till the going down thereof,"[79] so that there may be no cessation of the hymn of praise and thanksgiving which man owes to God, seeing that he required His help continually and has need of the blood of the Redeemer to remit sin which challenges God's justice.

II. The Participation of the Faithful in Offering the Eucharistic Sacrifice

80. It is, therefore, desirable, Venerable Brethren, that all the faithful should be aware that to participate in the eucharistic sacrifice is their chief duty and supreme dignity, and that not in an inert and negligent fashion, giving way to distractions and day-dreaming, but with such earnestness and concentration that they may be united as closely as possible with the High Priest, according to the Apostle, "Let this mind be in you which was also in Christ Jesus."[80] And together with Him and through Him let them make their oblation, and in union with Him let them offer up themselves.

81. It is quite true that Christ is a priest; but He is a priest not for Himself but for us, when in the name of the whole human race He offers our prayers and religious homage to the eternal Father; He is also a victim and for us since He substitutes Himself for sinful man. Now the exhortation of the Apostle, "Let this mind be in you which was also in Christ Jesus," requires that all Christians should possess, as far as is humanly possible, the same dispositions as those which the divine Redeemer had when He offered Himself in sacrifice: that is to say, they should in a humble attitude of mind, pay adoration, honour, praise and

---

[77] Cf. Sess. 22, c. 2. and can. 4.
[78] Cf. Gal. 6:14.
[79] Mal. 1:11.
[80] Phil. 2:5.

thanksgiving to the supreme majesty of God. Moreover, it means that they must assume to some extent the character of a victim, that they deny themselves as the Gospel commands, that freely and of their own accord they do penance and that each detests and satisfies for his sins. It means, in a word, that we must all undergo with Christ a mystical death on the cross so that we can apply to ourselves the words of St Paul, "With Christ I am nailed to the cross."[81]

82. The fact, however, that the faithful participate in the eucharistic sacrifice does not mean that they also are endowed with priestly power. It is very necessary that you make this quite clear to your flocks.

83. For there are today, Venerable Brethren, those who, approximating to errors long since condemned[82] teach that in the New Testament by the word "priesthood" is meant only that priesthood which applies to all who have been baptised; and hold that the command by which Christ gave power to His apostles at the Last Supper to do what He Himself had done, applies directly to the entire Christian Church, and that thence, and thence only, arises the hierarchical priesthood. Hence they assert that the people are possessed of a true priestly power, while the priest only acts in virtue of an office committed to him by the community. Wherefore, they look on the eucharistic sacrifice as a "concelebration," in the literal meaning of that term, and consider it more fitting that priests should "concelebrate" with the people present than that they should offer the sacrifice privately when the people are absent.

84. It is superfluous to explain how captious errors of this sort completely contradict the truths which We have just stated above, when treating of the place of the priest in the Mystical Body of Jesus Christ. But We deem it necessary to recall that the priest acts for the people only because he represents Jesus Christ, who is Head of all His members and offers Himself in their stead. Hence,

---

[81] Gal. 2:19.
[82] Cf. Council of Trent, Sess. 23. c. 4.

he goes to the altar as the minister of Christ, inferior to Christ but superior to the people.[83] The people, on the other hand, since they in no sense represent the divine Redeemer and are not mediator between themselves and God, can in no way possess the sacerdotal power.

85. All this has the certitude of faith. However, it must also be said that the faithful do offer the divine Victim, though in a different sense.

86. This has already been stated in the clearest terms by some of Our predecessors and some Doctors of the Church. "Not only," says Innocent III of immortal memory, "do the priests offer the sacrifice, but also all the faithful: for what the priest does personally by virtue of his ministry, the faithful do collectively by virtue of their intention."[84] We are happy to recall one of St Robert Bellarmine's many statements on this subject. "The sacrifice," he says "is principally offered in the person of Christ. Thus the oblation that follows the consecration is a sort of attestation that the whole Church consents in the oblation made by Christ, and offers it along with Him."[85]

87. Moreover, the rites and prayers of the eucharistic sacrifice signify and show no less clearly that the oblation of the Victim is made by the priests in company with the people. For not only does the sacred minister, after the oblation of the bread and wine when he turns to the people, say the significant prayer: "Pray brethren, that my sacrifice and yours may be acceptable to God the Father Almighty;"[86] but also the prayers by which the divine Victim is offered to God are generally expressed in the plural number: and in these it is indicated more than once that the people also participate in this august sacrifice inasmuch as they offer the same. The following words, for example, are used: "For whom we offer, or who offer up to Thee...We therefore beseech

---

[83] Cf. Saint Robert Bellarmine, *De Missa*, 2, c.4.

[84] *De Sacro Altaris Mysterio*, 3:6.

[85] *De Missa*, 1, c. 27.

[86] *Missale Romanum*, Ordinary of the Mass.

thee, O Lord, to be appeased and to receive this offering of our bounded duty, as also of thy whole household...We thy servants, as also thy whole people...do offer unto thy most excellent majesty, of thine own gifts bestowed upon us, a pure victim, a holy victim, a spotless victim."[87]

88. Nor is it to be wondered at, that the faithful should be raised to this dignity. By the waters of baptism, as by common right, Christians are made members of the Mystical Body of Christ the Priest, and by the "character" which is imprinted on their souls, they are appointed to give worship to God. Thus they participate, according to their condition, in the priesthood of Christ.

89. In every age of the Church's history, the mind of man, enlightened by faith, has aimed at the greatest possible knowledge of things divine. It is fitting, then, that the Christian people should also desire to know in what sense they are said in the canon of the Mass to offer up the sacrifice. To satisfy such a pious desire, then, We shall here explain the matter briefly and concisely.

90. First of all the more extrinsic explanations are these: it frequently happens that the faithful assisting at Mass join their prayers alternately with those of the priest, and sometimes - a more frequent occurrence in ancient times - they offer to the ministers at the altar bread and wine to be changed into the body and blood of Christ, and, finally, by their alms they get the priest to offer the divine victim for their intentions.

91. But there is also a more profound reason why all Christians, especially those who are present at Mass, are said to offer the sacrifice.

92. In this most important subject it is necessary, in order to avoid giving rise to a dangerous error, that we define the exact meaning of the word "offer." The unbloody immolation at the words of consecration, when Christ is made present upon the altar in the

---

[87] Ibid., Canon of the Mass.

state of a victim, is performed by the priest and by him alone, as the representative of Christ and not as the representative of the faithful. But it is because the priest places the divine victim upon the altar that he offers it to God the Father as an oblation for the glory of the Blessed Trinity and for the good of the whole Church. Now the faithful participate in the oblation, understood in this limited sense, after their own fashion and in a twofold manner, namely, because they not only offer the sacrifice by the hands of the priest, but also, to a certain extent, in union with him. It is by reason of this participation that the offering made by the people is also included in liturgical worship.

93. Now it is clear that the faithful offer the sacrifice by the hands of the priest from the fact that the minister at the altar, in offering a sacrifice in the name of all His members, represents Christ, the Head of the Mystical Body. Hence the whole Church can rightly be said to offer up the victim through Christ. But the conclusion that the people offer the sacrifice with the priest himself is not based on the fact that, being members of the Church no less than the priest himself, they perform a visible liturgical rite; for this is the privilege only of the minister who has been divinely appointed to this office: rather it is based on the fact that the people unite their hearts in praise, impetration, expiation and thanksgiving with prayers or intention of the priest, even of the High Priest himself, so that in the one and same offering of the victim and according to a visible sacerdotal rite, they may be presented to God the Father. It is obviously necessary that the external sacrificial rite should, of its very nature, signify the internal worship of the heart. Now the sacrifice of the New Law signifies that supreme worship by which the principal Offerer himself, who is Christ, and, in union with Him and through Him, all the members of the Mystical Body pay God the honour and reverence that are due to Him.

94. We are very pleased to learn that this teaching, thanks to a more intense study of the liturgy on the part of many, especially in recent years, has been given full recognition. We must, however, deeply deplore certain exaggerations and over-

statements which are not in agreement with the true teaching of the Church.

95. Some in fact disapprove altogether of those Masses which are offered privately and without any congregation, on the ground that they are a departure from the ancient way of offering the sacrifice; moreover, there are some who assert that priests cannot offer Mass at different altars at the same time, because, by doing so, they separate the community of the faithful and imperil its unity; while some go so far as to hold that the people must confirm and ratify the sacrifice if it is to have its proper force and value.

96. They are mistaken in appealing in this matter to the social character of the eucharistic sacrifice, for as often as a priest repeats what the divine Redeemer did at the Last Supper, the sacrifice is really completed. Moreover, this sacrifice, necessarily and of its very nature, has always and everywhere the character of a public and social act, inasmuch as he who offers it acts in the name of Christ and of the faithful, whose Head is the divine Redeemer, and he offers it to God for the holy Catholic Church, and for the living and the dead.[88] This is undoubtedly so, whether the faithful are present - as we desire and commend them to be in great numbers and with devotion - or are not present, since it is in no wise required that the people ratify what the sacred minister has done.

97. Still, though it is clear from what We have said that the Mass is offered in the name of Christ and of the Church and that it is not robbed of its social effects though it be celebrated by a priest without a server, nonetheless, on account of the dignity of such an august mystery, it is Our earnest desire - as Mother Church has always commanded - that no priest should say Mass unless a server is at hand to answer the prayers, as canon 813 prescribes.

98. In order that the oblation by which the faithful offer the divine Victim in this sacrifice to the Heavenly Father may have its full

---

[88] Ibid..

effect, it is necessary that the people add something else, namely, the offering of themselves as a victim.

99. This offering in fact is not confined merely to the liturgical sacrifice. For the Prince of the Apostles wishes us, as living stones built upon Christ, the cornerstone, to be able as "a holy priesthood, to offer up spiritual sacrifices, acceptable to God by Jesus Christ."[89] St Paul the Apostle addresses the following words of exhortation to Christians, without distinction of time, "I beseech you therefore, . . . that you present your bodies, a living sacrifice, holy, pleasing unto God, your reasonable service."[90] But at that time especially when the faithful take part in the liturgical service with such piety and recollection that it can truly be said of them: "whose faith and devotion is known to Thee,"[91] it is then, with the High Priest and through Him they offer themselves as a spiritual sacrifice, that each one's faith ought to become more ready to work through charity, his piety more real and fervent, and each one should consecrate himself to the furthering of the divine glory, desiring to become as like as possible to Christ in His most grievous sufferings.

100. This we are also taught by those exhortations which the Bishop, in the Church's name, addresses to priests on the day of their ordination, "Understand what you do, imitate what you handle, and since you celebrate the mystery of the Lord's death, take good care to mortify your members with their vices and concupiscences."[92] In almost the same manner the sacred books of the liturgy advise Christians who come to Mass to participate in the sacrifice: "At this...altar let innocence be in honour, let pride be sacrificed, anger slain, impurity and every evil desire laid low, let the sacrifice of chastity be offered in place of doves and instead of the young pigeons the sacrifice of innocence."[93] While we stand before the altar, then, it is our duty so to

---

[89] 1 Peter, 2:5.

[90] Rom. 12:1.

[91] *Missale Romanum*, Canon of the Mass.

[92] *Pontificale Romanum*, Ordination of a priest.

[93] Ibid., Consecration of an altar, Preface.

transform our hearts, that every trace of sin may be completely blotted out, while whatever promotes supernatural life through Christ may be zealously fostered and strengthened even to the extent that, in union with the immaculate Victim, we become a victim acceptable to the eternal Father.

101. The prescriptions in fact of the Sacred Liturgy aim, by every means at their disposal, at helping the Church to bring about this most holy purpose in the most suitable manner possible. This is the object not only of readings, homilies and other sermons given by priests, as also the whole cycle of mysteries which are proposed for our commemoration in the course of the year, but it is also the purpose of vestments, of sacred rites and their external splendour. All these things aim at "enhancing the majesty of this great Sacrifice, and raising the minds of the faithful by means of these visible signs of religion and piety, to the contemplation of the sublime truths contained in this sacrifice."[94]

102. All the elements of the liturgy, then, would have us reproduce in our hearts the likeness of the divine Redeemer through the mystery of the cross, according to the words of the Apostle of the Gentiles, "With Christ I am nailed to the cross. I live, now not I, but Christ liveth in me."[95] Thus we become a victim, as it were, along with Christ to increase the glory of the eternal Father.

103. Let this, then, be the intention and aspiration of the faithful, when they offer up the divine Victim in the Mass. For if, as St Augustine writes, our mystery is enacted on the Lord's table, that is Christ our Lord Himself,[96] who is the Head and symbol of that union through which we are the body of Christ[97] and members of His Body;[98] if St Robert Bellarmine teaches, according to the mind of the Doctor of Hippo, that in the sacrifice of the altar there is

---

[94] Cf. Council of Trent, Sess. 22, c. 5.
[95] Gal. 2:19-20.
[96] Cf. *Serm.* 272.
[97] Cf. 1 Cor. 12:27.
[98] Cf. Eph. 5:30.

signified the general sacrifice by which the whole Mystical Body of Christ, that is, all the city of redeemed, is offered up to God through Christ, the High Priest:[99] nothing can be conceived more just or fitting than that all of us in union with our Head, who suffered for our sake, should also sacrifice ourselves to the eternal Father. For in the sacrament of the altar, as the same St Augustine has it, the Church is made to see that in what she offers she herself is offered.[100]

104. Let the faithful, therefore, consider to what a high dignity they are raised by the sacrament of baptism. They should not think it enough to participate in the eucharistic sacrifice with that general intention which befits members of Christ and children of the Church, but let them further, in keeping with the spirit of the Sacred Liturgy, be most closely united with the High Priest and His earthly minister, at the time the consecration of the divine Victim is enacted, and at that time especially when those solemn words are pronounced, "By Him and with Him and in Him is to Thee, God the Father almighty, in the unity of the Holy Ghost, all honour and glory for ever and ever;"[101] to these words in fact the people answer, "Amen." Nor should Christians forget to offer themselves, their cares, their sorrows, their distress and their necessities in union with their divine Saviour upon the cross.

105. Therefore, they are to be praised who, with the idea of getting the Christian people to take part more easily and more fruitfully in the Mass, strive to make them familiar with the "Roman Missal," so that the faithful, united with the priest, may pray together in the very words and sentiments of the Church. They also are to be commended who strive to make the liturgy even in an external way a sacred act in which all who are present may share. This can be done in more than one way, when, for instance, the whole congregation, in accordance with the rules of the liturgy, either answer the priest in an orderly and fitting manner, or sing hymns suitable to the different parts of the Mass,

---

[99] Cf. Saint Robert Bellarmine, *De Missa*, 2, c. 8.

[100] Cf. *De Civitate Dei*, Book 10, c. 6.

[101] *Missale Romanum*, Canon of the Mass.

or do both, or finally in high Masses when they answer the prayers of the minister of Jesus Christ and also sing the liturgical chant.

106. These methods of participation in the Mass are to be approved and recommended when they are in complete agreement with the precepts of the Church and the rubrics of the liturgy. Their chief aim is to foster and promote the people's piety and intimate union with Christ and His visible minister and to arouse those internal sentiments and dispositions which should make our hearts become like to that of the High Priest of the New Testament. However, though they show also in an outward manner that the very nature of the sacrifice, as offered by the Mediator between God and men,[102] must be regarded as the act of the whole Mystical Body of Christ, still they are by no means necessary to constitute it a public act or to give it a social character. And besides, a "dialogue" Mass of this kind cannot replace the high Mass, which, as a matter of fact, though it should be offered with only the sacred ministers present, possesses its own special dignity due to the impressive character of its ritual and the magnificence of its ceremonies. The splendour and grandeur of a high Mass, however, are very much increased if, as the Church desires, the people are present in great numbers and with devotion.

107. It is to be observed, also, that they have strayed from the path of truth and right reason who, led away by false opinions, make so much of these accidentals as to presume to assert that without them the Mass cannot fulfil its appointed end.

108. Many of the faithful are unable to use the Roman missal even though it is written in the vernacular; nor are all capable of understanding correctly the liturgical rites and formulas. So varied and diverse are men's talents and characters that it is impossible for all to be moved and attracted to the same extent by community prayers, hymns and liturgical services. Moreover, the needs and inclinations of all are not the same, nor are they always

---

[102] Cf. 1 Tim. 2:5.

constant in the same individual. Who, then, would say, on account of such a prejudice, that all these Christians cannot participate in the Mass nor share its fruits? On the contrary, they can adopt some other method which proves easier for certain people; for instance, they can lovingly meditate on the mysteries of Jesus Christ or perform other exercises of piety or recite prayers which, though they differ from the sacred rites, are still essentially in harmony with them.

109. Wherefore We exhort you, Venerable Brethren, that each in his diocese or ecclesiastical jurisdiction supervise and regulate the manner and method in which the people take part in the liturgy, according to the rubrics of the missal and in keeping with the injunctions which the Sacred Congregation of Rites and the Code of canon law have published. Let everything be done with due order and dignity, and let no one, not even a priest, make use of the sacred edifices according to his whim to try out experiments. It is also Our wish that in each diocese an advisory committee to promote the liturgical apostolate should be established, similar to that which cares for sacred music and art, so that with your watchful guidance everything may be carefully carried out in accordance with the prescriptions of the Apostolic See.

110. In religious communities let all those regulations be accurately observed which are laid down in their respective constitutions, nor let any innovations be made which the superiors of these communities have not previously approved.

111. But however much variety and disparity there may be in the exterior manner and circumstances in which the Christian laity participate in the Mass and other liturgical functions, constant and earnest effort must be made to unite the congregation in spirit as much as possible with the divine Redeemer, so that their lives may be daily enriched with more abundant sanctity, and greater glory be given to the Heavenly Father.

III. Holy Communion

112. The august sacrifice of the altar is concluded with communion or the partaking of the divine feast. But, as all know, the integrity of the sacrifice only requires that the priest partake of the heavenly food. Although it is most desirable that the people should also approach the holy table, this is not required for the integrity of the sacrifice.

113. We wish in this matter to repeat the remarks which Our predecessor Benedict XIV makes with regard to the definitions of the Council of Trent: "First We must state that none of the faithful can hold that private Masses, in which the priest alone receives holy communion, are therefore unlawful and do not fulfil the idea of the true, perfect and complete unbloody sacrifice instituted by Christ our Lord. For the faithful know quite well, or at least can easily be taught, that the Council of Trent, supported by the doctrine which the uninterrupted tradition of the Church has preserved, condemned the new and false opinion of Luther as opposed to this tradition."[103] "If anyone shall say that Masses in which the priest only receives communion, are unlawful, and therefore should be abolished, let him be anathema."[104]

114. They, therefore, err from the path of truth who do not want to have Masses celebrated unless the faithful communicate; and those are still more in error who, in holding that it is altogether necessary for the faithful to receive holy communion as well as the priest, put forward the captious argument that here there is question not of a sacrifice merely, but of a sacrifice and a supper of brotherly union, and consider the general communion of all present as the culminating point of the whole celebration.

115. Now it cannot be over-emphasised that the eucharistic sacrifice of its very nature is the unbloody immolation of the divine Victim, which is made manifest in a mystical manner by the separation of the sacred species and by their oblation to the

---

[103] Encyclical Letter *Certiores effecti*, November 13, 1742, par. 1.
[104] Council of Trent, Sess. 22, can. 8.

eternal Father. Holy communion pertains to the integrity of the Mass and to the partaking of the august sacrament; but while it is obligatory for the priest who says the Mass, it is only something earnestly recommended to the faithful.

116. The Church, as the teacher of truth, strives by every means in her power to safeguard the integrity of the Catholic faith, and like a mother solicitous for the welfare of her children, she exhorts them most earnestly to partake fervently and frequently of the richest treasure of our religion.

117. She wishes in the first place that Christians - especially when they cannot easily receive holy communion - should do so at least by desire, so that with renewed faith, reverence, humility and complete trust in the goodness of the divine Redeemer, they may be united to Him in the spirit of the most ardent charity.

118. But the desire of Mother Church does not stop here. For since by feasting upon the Bread of Angels we can by a "sacramental" communion, as We have already said, also become partakers of the sacrifice, she repeats the invitation to all her children individually, "Take and eat. . . Do this in memory of Me"[105] so that "we may continually experience within us the fruit of our redemption"[106] in a more efficacious manner. For this reason the Council of Trent, re-echoing, as it were, the invitation of Christ and His immaculate Spouse, has earnestly exhorted "the faithful when they attend Mass to communicate not only by a spiritual communion but also by a sacramental one, so that they may obtain more abundant fruit from this most holy sacrifice."[107] Moreover, Our predecessor of immortal memory, Benedict XIV, wishing to emphasise and throw fuller light upon the truth that the faithful by receiving the Holy Eucharist become partakers of the divine sacrifice itself, praises the devotion of those who, when attending Mass, not only elicit a desire to receive holy communion but also want to be nourished by hosts consecrated

---

[105] 1 Cor. 11:24.
[106] *Missale Romanum*, Collect for Feast of Corpus Christi.
[107] Sess. 22, c. 6.

during the Mass, even though, as he himself states, they really and truly take part in the sacrifice should they receive a host which has been duly consecrated at a previous Mass. He writes as follows: "And although in addition to those to whom the celebrant gives a portion of the Victim he himself has offered in the Mass, they also participate in the same sacrifice to whom a priest distributes the Blessed Sacrament that has been reserved; however, the Church has not for this reason ever forbidden, nor does she now forbid, a celebrant to satisfy the piety and just request of those who, when present at Mass, want to become partakers of the same sacrifice, because they likewise offer it after their own manner, nay more, she approves of it and desires that it should not be omitted and would reprehend those priests through whose fault and negligence this participation would be denied to the faithful."[108]

119. May God grant that all accept these invitations of the Church freely and with spontaneity. May He grant that they participate even every day, if possible, in the divine sacrifice, not only in a spiritual manner, but also by reception of the august sacrament, receiving the body of Jesus Christ which has been offered for all to the eternal Father. Arouse Venerable Brethren, in the hearts of those committed to your care, a great and insatiable hunger for Jesus Christ. Under your guidance let the children and youth crowd to the altar rails to offer themselves, their innocence and their works of zeal to the divine Redeemer. Let husbands and wives approach the holy table so that nourished on this food they may learn to make the children entrusted to them conformed to the mind and heart of Jesus Christ.

120. Let the workers be invited to partake of this sustaining and never failing nourishment that it may renew their strength and obtain for their labours an everlasting recompense in heaven; in a word, invite all men of whatever class and compel them to come in;[109] since this is the Bread of Life which all require. The Church of Jesus Christ needs no other bread than this to satisfy fully our

---

[108] Encyclical Letter *Certiores effecti*, par. 3.
[109] Cf. Luke, 14:23.

souls' wants and desires, and to unite us in the most intimate union with Jesus Christ, to make us "one body,"[110] to get us to live together as brothers who, breaking the same bread, sit down to the same heavenly table, to partake of the elixir of immortality.[111]

121. Now it is very fitting, as the liturgy otherwise lays down, that the people receive holy communion after the priest has partaken of the divine repast upon the altar; and, as We have written above, they should be commended who, when present at Mass, receive hosts consecrated at the same Mass, so that it is actually verified, "that as many of us, as, at this altar, shall partake of and receive the most holy body and blood of thy Son, may be filled with every heavenly blessing and grace."[112]

122. Still sometimes there may be a reason, and that not infrequently, why holy communion should be distributed before or after Mass and even immediately after the priest receives the sacred species - and even though hosts consecrated at a previous Mass should be used. In these circumstances - as We have stated above - the people duly take part in the eucharistic sacrifice and not seldom they can in this way more conveniently receive holy communion. Still, though the Church with the kind heart of a mother strives to meet the spiritual needs of her children, they, for their part, should not readily neglect the directions of the liturgy and, as often as there is no reasonable difficulty, should aim that all their actions at the altar manifest more clearly the living unity of the Mystical Body.

123. When the Mass, which is subject to special rules of the liturgy, is over, the person who has received holy communion is not thereby freed from his duty of thanksgiving; rather, it is most becoming that, when the Mass is finished, the person who has received the Eucharist should recollect himself, and in intimate union with the divine Master hold loving and fruitful converse

---

[110] 1 Cor. 10:17.

[111] Cf. Saint Ignatius of Antioch, *Ad Eph.* 20.

[112] *Missale Romanum,* Canon of the Mass.

with Him. Hence they have departed from the straight way of truth, who, adhering to the letter rather than the sense, assert and teach that, when Mass has ended, no such thanksgiving should be added, not only because the Mass is itself a thanksgiving, but also because this pertains to a private and personal act of piety and not to the good of the community.

124. But, on the contrary, the very nature of the sacrament demands that its reception should produce rich fruits of Christian sanctity. Admittedly the congregation has been officially dismissed, but each individual, since he is united with Christ, should not interrupt the hymn of praise in his own soul, "always returning thanks for all in the name of our Lord Jesus Christ to God the Father."[113] The Sacred Liturgy of the Mass also exhorts us to do this when it bids us pray in these words, "Grant, we beseech thee, that we may always continue to offer thanks[114] ...and may never cease from praising thee."[115] Wherefore, if there is no time when we must not offer God thanks, and if we must never cease from praising Him, who would dare to reprehend or find fault with the Church, because she advises her priests[116] and faithful to converse with the divine Redeemer for at least a short while after holy communion, and inserts in her liturgical books, fitting prayers, enriched with indulgences, by which the sacred ministers may make suitable preparation before Mass and holy communion or may return thanks afterwards? So far is the Sacred Liturgy from restricting the interior devotion of individual Christians, that it actually fosters and promotes it so that they may be rendered like to Jesus Christ and through Him be brought to the Heavenly Father; wherefore this same discipline of the liturgy demands that whoever has partaken of the sacrifice of the altar should return fitting thanks to God. For it is the good pleasure of the divine Redeemer to hearken to us when we pray,

---

[113] Eph. 5:20.

[114] *Missale Romanum*, Postcommunion for Sunday within the Octave of Ascension.

[115] Ibid., Postcommunion for First Sunday after Pentecost.

[116] Code of Canon Law, can. 810.

to converse with us intimately and to offer us a refuge in His loving Heart.

125. Moreover, such personal colloquies are very necessary that we may all enjoy more fully the supernatural treasures that are contained in the Eucharist and according to our means, share them with others, so that Christ our Lord may exert the greatest possible influence on the souls of all.

126. Why then, Venerable Brethren, should We not approve of those who, when they receive holy communion, remain on in closest familiarity with their divine Redeemer even after the congregation has been officially dismissed, and that not only for the consolation of conversing with Him, but also to render Him due thanks and praise and especially to ask help to defend their souls against anything that may lessen the efficacy of the sacrament and to do everything in their power to cooperate with the action of Christ who is so intimately present. We exhort them to do so in a special manner by carrying out their resolutions, by exercising the Christian virtues, as also by applying to their own necessities the riches they have received with royal Liberality. The author of that golden book *The Imitation of Christ* certainly speaks in accordance with the letter and the spirit of the liturgy, when he gives the following advice to the person who approaches the altar, "Remain on in secret and take delight in your God; for He is yours whom the whole world cannot take away from you."[117]

127. Therefore, let us all enter into closest union with Christ and strive to lose ourselves, as it were, in His most holy soul and so be united to Him that we may have a share in those acts with which He adores the Blessed Trinity with a homage that is most acceptable, and by which He offers to the eternal Father supreme praise and thanks which find an harmonious echo throughout the heavens and the earth, according to the words of the prophet, "All ye works of the Lord, bless the Lord."[118] Finally, in union

---

[117] Book IV, c. 12
[118] Dan. 3:57.

with these sentiments of Christ, let us ask for heavenly aid at that moment in which it is supremely fitting to pray for and obtain help in His name.[119] For it is especially in virtue of these sentiments that we offer and immolate ourselves as a victim, saying, "make of us thy eternal offering."[120]

128. The divine Redeemer is ever repeating His pressing invitation, "Abide in Me."[121] Now by the sacrament of the Eucharist, Christ remains in us and we in Him, and just as Christ, remaining in us, lives and works, so should we remain in Christ and live and work through Him.

IV. Adoration of the Eucharist

129. The Eucharistic Food contains, as all are aware, "truly, really and substantially the Body and Blood together with soul and divinity of our Lord Jesus Christ."[122] It is no wonder, then, that the Church, even from the beginning, adored the body of Christ under the appearance of bread; this is evident from the very rites of the august sacrifice, which prescribe that the sacred ministers should adore the most holy sacrament by genuflecting or by profoundly bowing their heads.

130. The Sacred Councils teach that it is the Church's tradition right from the beginning, to worship "with the same adoration the Word Incarnate as well as His own flesh,"[123] and St Augustine asserts that, "No one eats that flesh, without first adoring it," while he adds that "not only do we not commit a sin by adoring it, but that we do sin by not adoring it."[124]

---

[119] Cf. John 16: 3.
[120] *Missale Romanum,* Secret for Mass of the Most Blessed Trinity.
[121] John, 15:4.
[122] Council of Trent, Sess. 13, can. 1.
[123] Second Council of Constantinople, *Anath, de trib. Capit.,* can. 9; compare Council of Ephesus, *Anath. Cyrill,* can 8. Cf. Council of Trent, Sess. 13, can. 6; Pius VI Constitution *Auctorem fidei,* n. 61.
[124] Cf. *Enarr in Ps.* 98:9.

131. It is on this doctrinal basis that the cult of adoring the Eucharist was founded and gradually developed as something distinct from the sacrifice of the Mass. The reservation of the sacred species for the sick and those in danger of death introduced the praiseworthy custom of adoring the Blessed Sacrament which is reserved in our churches. This practice of adoration, in fact, is based on strong and solid reasons. For the Eucharist is at once a sacrifice and a sacrament; but it differs from the other sacraments in this that it not only produces grace, but contains in a permanent manner the Author of grace Himself. When, therefore, the Church bids us adore Christ hidden behind the eucharistic veils and pray to Him for spiritual and temporal favours, of which we ever stand in need, she manifests living faith in her divine Spouse who is present beneath these veils, she professes her gratitude to Him and she enjoys the intimacy of His friendship.

132. Now, the Church in the course of centuries has introduced various forms of this worship which are ever increasing in beauty and helpfulness: as, for example, visits of devotion to the tabernacles, even every day; Benediction of the Blessed Sacrament; solemn processions, especially at the time of Eucharistic Congress, which pass through cities and villages; and adoration of the Blessed Sacrament publicly exposed. Sometimes these public acts of adoration are of short duration. Sometimes they last for one, several and even for forty hours. In certain places they continue in turn in different churches throughout the year, while elsewhere adoration is perpetual day and night, under the care of religious communities, and the faithful quite often take part in them.

133. These exercises of piety have brought a wonderful increase in faith and supernatural life to the Church militant upon earth and they are re-echoed to a certain extent by the Church triumphant in heaven which sings continually a hymn of praise to God and to the Lamb "who was slain."[125] Wherefore, the Church not merely approves these pious practices, which in the

---

[125] Apoc. 5:12, cp. 7:10.

course of centuries have spread everywhere throughout the world, but makes them her own, as it were, and by her authority commends them.[126] They spring from the inspiration of the liturgy and if they are performed with due propriety and with faith and piety, as the liturgical rules of the Church require, they are undoubtedly of the very greatest assistance in living the life of the liturgy.

134. Nor is it to be admitted that by this Eucharistic cult men falsely confound the historical Christ, as they say, who once lived on earth, with the Christ who is present in the august Sacrament of the altar, and who reigns glorious and triumphant in heaven and bestows supernatural favours. On the contrary, it can be claimed that by this devotion the faithful bear witness to and solemnly avow the faith of the Church that the Word of God is identical with the Son of the Virgin Mary, who suffered on the cross, who is present in a hidden manner in the Eucharist and who reigns upon His heavenly throne. Thus, St John Chrysostom states: "When you see It [the Body of Christ] exposed, say to yourself: Thanks to this body, I am no longer dust and ashes, I am no more a captive but a freeman: hence I hope to obtain heaven and the good things that are there in store for me, eternal life, the heritage of the angels, companionship with Christ; death has not destroyed this body which was pierced by nails and scourged,…this is that body which was once covered with blood, pierced by a lance, from which issued saving fountains upon the world, one of blood and the other of water…This body He gave to us to keep and eat, as a mark of His intense love."[127]

135. That practice in a special manner is to be highly praised according to which many exercises of piety, customary among the faithful, and with Benediction of the Blessed Sacrament. For excellent and of great benefit is that custom which makes the priest raise aloft the Bread of Angels before congregations with heads bowed down in adoration, and forming with It the sign of the cross implores the Heavenly Father to deign to look upon His

---

[126] Cf. Council of Trent, Sess. 13, c. 5 and can. 6.
[127] *In I ad Cor.*, 24:4.

Son who for love of us was nailed to the cross, and for His sake and through Him who willed to be our Redeemer and our brother, be pleased to shower down heavenly favours upon those whom the immaculate blood of the Lamb has redeemed.[128]

136. Strive then, Venerable Brethren, with your customary devoted care so the churches, which the faith and piety of Christian peoples have built in the course of centuries for the purpose of singing a perpetual hymn of glory to God almighty and of providing a worthy abode for our Redeemer concealed beneath the eucharistic species, may be entirely at the disposal of greater numbers of the faithful who, called to the feet of their Saviour, hearken to His most consoling invitation, "Come to Me all you who labour and are heavily burdened, and I will refresh you."[129] Let your churches be the house of God where all who enter to implore blessings rejoice in obtaining whatever they ask[130] and find there heavenly consolation.

137. Only thus can it be brought about that the whole human family settling their differences may find peace, and united in mind and heart may sing this song of hope and charity, "Good Pastor, truly bread - Jesus have mercy on us - feed us, protect us - bestow on us the vision of all good things in the land of the living."[131]

---

[128] Cf. 1 Peter, 1:19.
[129] Matt. 11:28.
[130] Cf. *Missale Romanum*, Collect for Mass for the Dedication of a Church.
[131] Ibid., Sequence *Lauda Sion* in Mass for Feast of Corpus Christi.

PART III
THE DIVINE OFFICE AND THE LITURGICAL YEAR

I. The Divine Office

138. The ideal of Christian life is that each one be united to God in the closest and most intimate manner. For this reason, the worship that the Church renders to God, and which is based especially on the eucharistic sacrifice and the use of the sacraments, is directed and arranged in such a way that it embraces by means of the Divine Office, the hours of the day, the weeks and the whole cycle of the year, and reaches all the aspects and phases of human life.

139. Since the divine Master commanded "that we ought always to pray and not to faint,"[132] the Church faithfully fulfils this injunction and never ceases to pray: she urges us in the words of the Apostle of the Gentiles, "by him Jesus let us offer the sacrifice of praise always to God."[133]

140. Public and common prayer offered to God by all at the same time was customary in antiquity only on certain days and at certain times. Indeed, people prayed to God not only in groups but in private houses and occasionally with neighbours and friends. But soon in different parts of the Christian world the practice arose of setting aside special times for praying, as for example, the last hour of the day when evening set in and the lamps were lighted; or the first, heralded, when the night was coming to an end, by the crowing of the cock and the rising of the morning star. Other times of the day, as being more suitable for prayer are indicated in Sacred Scripture, in Hebrew customs or in keeping with the practice of every-day life. According to the Acts of the Apostles, the disciples of Jesus Christ all came together to pray at the third hour, when they were all filled with the Holy

---

[132] Luke, 18:1.
[133] Heb. 13:15.

Ghost;[134] and before eating, the Prince of the Apostles went up to the higher parts of the house to pray, about the sixth hour;[135] Peter and John "went up into the Temple at the ninth hour of prayer"[136] and at "midnight Paul and Silas praying . . . praised God."[137]

141. Thanks to the work of the monks and those who practice asceticism, these various prayers in the course of time become ever more perfected and by the authority of the Church are gradually incorporated into the Sacred Liturgy.

142. The Divine Office is the prayer of the Mystical Body of Jesus Christ, offered to God in the name and on behalf of all Christians, when recited by priests and other ministers of the Church and by religious who are deputed by the Church for this.

143. The character and value of the Divine Office may be gathered from the words recommended by the Church to be said before starting the prayers of the office, namely, that they be said "worthily, with attention and devotion."

144. By assuming human nature, the Divine Word introduced into this earthly exile a hymn which is sung in heaven for all eternity. He unites to Himself the whole human race and with it sings this hymn to the praise of God. As we must humbly recognise that "we know not what we should pray for, as we ought, the Spirit Himself asketh for us with unspeakable groanings."[138] Moreover, through His Spirit in us, Christ entreats the Father, "God could not give a greater gift to men...[Jesus] prays for us, as our Priest; He prays in us as our Head; we pray to Him as our God...we recognise in Him our voice and His voice in us...He is prayed to as God, He prays under the appearance of a servant; in heaven He is Creator; here, created though not

---

134 Cf. Acts, 2:1-15.
135 Ibid., 10:9.
136 Ibid., 3:1.
137 Ibid., 16:25.
138 Rom. 8:26.

changed, He assumes a created nature which is to be changed and makes us with Him one complete man, head and body."[139]

145. To this lofty dignity of the Church's prayer, there should correspond earnest devotion in our souls. For when in prayer the voice repeats those hymns written under the inspiration of the Holy Ghost and extols God's infinite perfections, it is necessary that the interior sentiment of our souls should accompany the voice so as to make those sentiments our own in which we are elevated to heaven, adoring and giving due praise and thanks to the Blessed Trinity; "so let us chant in choir that mind and voice may accord together."[140] It is not merely a question of recitation or of singing which, however perfect according to norms of music and the sacred rites, only reaches the ear, but it is especially a question of the ascent of the mind and heart to God so that, united with Christ, we may completely dedicate ourselves and all our actions to Him.

146. On this depends in no small way the efficacy of our prayers. These prayers in fact, when they are not addressed directly to the Word made man, conclude with the phrase "through Jesus Christ our Lord." As our Mediator with God, He shows to the Heavenly Father His glorified wounds, "always living to make intercessions for us."[141]

147. The Psalms, as all know, form the chief part of the Divine Office. They encompass the full round of the day and sanctify it. Cassiodorus speaks beautifully about the Psalms as distributed in his day throughout the Divine Office: "With the celebration of matins they bring a blessing on the coming day, they set aside for us the first hour and consecrate the third hour of the day, they gladden the sixth hour with the breaking of bread, at the ninth

---

[139] Saint Augustine, *Enarr. in Ps.* 85, n. 1.
[140] Saint Benedict, *Regula Monachorum*, c. 19.
[141] Heb. 7:25.

they terminate our fast, they bring the evening to a close and at nightfall they shield our minds from darkness."[142]

148. The Psalms recall to mind the truths revealed by God to the chosen people, which were at one time frightening and at another filled with wonderful tenderness; they keep repeating and fostering the hope of the promised Liberator which in ancient times was kept alive with song, either around the hearth or in the stately temple; they show forth in splendid light the prophesied glory of Jesus Christ: first, His supreme and eternal power, then His lowly coming to this terrestrial exile, His kingly dignity and priestly power and, finally, His beneficent labours, and the shedding of His blood for our redemption. In a similar way they express the joy, the bitterness, the hope and fear of our hearts and our desire of loving God and hoping in Him alone, and our mystic ascent to divine tabernacles.

149. "The psalm is…a blessing for the people, it is the praise of God, the tribute of the nation, the common language and acclamation of all, it is the voice of the Church, the harmonious confession of faith, signifying deep attachment to authority; it is the joy of freedom, the expression of happiness, an echo of bliss."[143]

150. In an earlier age, these canonical prayers were attended by many of the faithful. But this gradually ceased, and, as We have already said, their recitation at present is the duty only of the clergy and of religious. The laity have no obligation in this matter. Still, it is greatly to be desired that they participate in reciting or chanting vespers sung in their own parish on feast days. We earnestly exhort you, Venerable Brethren, to see that this pious practice is kept up, and that wherever it has ceased you restore it if possible. This, without doubt, will produce salutary results when vespers are conducted in a worthy and fitting

---

[142] *Explicatio in Psalterium,* Preface. Text as found in Migne, Parres Larini, 70:10. But some are of the opinion that part of this passage should not be attributed to Cassiodorus.

[143] Saint Ambrose, *Enarr in Ps.* 1, n. 9.

manner and with such helps as foster the piety of the faithful. Let the public and private observance of the feasts of the Church, which are in a special way dedicated and consecrated to God, be kept inviolable; and especially the Lord's day which the Apostles, under the guidance of the Holy Ghost, substituted for the sabbath. Now, if the order was given to the Jews: "Six days shall you do work; in the seventh day is the sabbath, the rest holy to the Lord. Every one that shall do any work on this day, shall die;"[144] how will these Christians not fear spiritual death who perform servile work on feast-days, and whose rest on these days is not devoted to religion and piety but given over to the allurements of the world? Sundays and holy days, then, must be made holy by divine worship, which gives homage to God and heavenly food to the soul. Although the Church only commands the faithful to abstain from servile work and attend Mass and does not make it obligatory to attend evening devotions, still she desires this and recommends it repeatedly. Moreover, the needs of each one demand it, seeing that all are bound to win the favour of God if they are to obtain His benefits. Our soul is filled with the greatest grief when We see how the Christian people of today profane the afternoon of feast days; public places of amusement and public games are frequented in great numbers while the churches are not as full as they should be. All should come to our churches and there be taught the truth of the Catholic faith, sing the praises of God, be enriched with Benediction of the Blessed Sacrament given by the priest and be strengthened with help from heaven against the adversities of this life. Let all try to learn those prayers which are recited at vespers and fill their souls with their meaning. When deeply penetrated by these prayers, they will experience what St Augustine said about himself: "How much did I weep during hymns and verses, greatly moved at the sweet singing of thy Church. Their sound would penetrate my ears and their truth melt my heart, sentiments of piety would well up, tears would flow and that was good for me."[145]

---

[144] Exod. 31:15.
[145] *Confessions*, Book 9, c. 6.

II. The Cycle of the Mysteries

151. Throughout the entire year, the Mass and the Divine Office centre especially around the person of Jesus Christ. This arrangement is so suitably disposed that our Saviour dominates the scene in the mysteries of His humiliation, of His redemption and triumph.

152. While the Sacred Liturgy calls to mind the mysteries of Jesus Christ, it strives to make all believers take their part in them so that the divine Head of the mystical Body may live in all the members with the fullness of His holiness. Let the souls of Christians be like altars on each one of which a different phase of the sacrifice, offered by the High priest, comes to life again, as it were: pains and tears which wipe away and expiate sin; supplication to God which pierces heaven; dedication and even immolation of oneself made promptly, generously and earnestly; and, finally, that intimate union by which we commit ourselves and all we have to God, in whom we find our rest. "The perfection of religion is to imitate whom you adore."[146]

153. By these suitable ways and methods in which the liturgy at stated times proposes the life of Jesus Christ for our meditation, the Church gives us examples to imitate, points out treasures of sanctity for us to make our own, since it is fitting that the mind believes what the lips sing, and that what the mind believes should be practised in public and private life.

154. In the period of Advent, for instance, the Church arouses in us the consciousness of the sins we have had the misfortune to commit, and urges us, by restraining our desires and practising voluntary mortification of the body, to recollect ourselves in meditation, and experience a longing desire to return to God who alone can free us by His grace from the stain of sin and from its evil consequences.

---

[146] Saint Augustine, *De Civitate Dei*, Book 8, c. 17.

155. With the coming of the birthday of the Redeemer, she would bring us to the cave of Bethlehem and there teach that we must be born again and undergo a complete reformation; that will only happen when we are intimately and vitally united to the Word of God made man and participate in His divine nature, to which we have been elevated.

156. At the solemnity of the Epiphany, in putting before us the call of the Gentiles to the Christian faith, she wishes us daily to give thanks to the Lord for such a blessing; she wishes us to seek with lively faith the living and true God, to penetrate deeply and religiously the things of heaven, to love silence and meditation in order to perceive and grasp more easily heavenly gifts.

157. During the days of Septuagesima and Lent, our Holy Mother the Church over and over again strives to make each of us seriously consider our misery, so that we may be urged to a practical emendation of our lives, detest our sins heartily and expiate them by prayer and penance. For constant prayer and penance done for past sins obtain for us divine help, without which every work of ours is useless and unavailing.

158. In Holy Week, when the most bitter sufferings of Jesus Christ are put before us by the liturgy, the Church invites us to come to Calvary and follow in the blood-stained footsteps of the divine Redeemer, to carry the cross willingly with Him, to reproduce in our own hearts His spirit of expiation and atonement, and to die together with Him.

159. At the Paschal season, which commemorates the triumph of Christ, our souls are filled with deep interior joy: we, accordingly, should also consider that we must rise, in union with the Redeemer, from our cold and slothful life to one of greater fervour and holiness by giving ourselves completely and generously to God, and by forgetting this wretched world in order to aspire only to the things of heaven: "If you be risen with

Christ, seek the things that are above...mind the things that are above."[147]

160. Finally, during the time of Pentecost, the Church by her precept and practice urges us to be more docile to the action of the Holy Spirit who wishes us to be on fire with divine love so that we may daily strive to advance more in virtue and thus become holy as Christ our Lord and His Father are holy.

161. Thus, the liturgical year should be considered as a splendid hymn of praise offered to the Heavenly Father by the Christian family through Jesus, their perpetual Mediator. Nevertheless, it requires a diligent and well ordered study on our part to be able to know and praise our Redeemer ever more and more. It requires a serious effort and constant practice to imitate His mysteries, to enter willingly upon His path of sorrow and thus finally share His glory and eternal happiness.

162. From what We have already explained, Venerable Brethren, it is perfectly clear how much modern writers are wanting in the genuine and true liturgical spirit who, deceived by the illusion of a higher mysticism, dare to assert that attention should be paid not to the historic Christ but to a "pneumatic" or glorified Christ. They do not hesitate to assert that a change has taken place in the piety of the faithful by dethroning, as it were, Christ from His position; since they say that the glorified Christ, who liveth and reigneth forever and sitteth at the right hand of the Father, has been overshadowed and in His place has been substituted that Christ who lived on earth. For this reason, some have gone so far as to want to remove from the churches images of the divine Redeemer suffering on the cross.

163. But these false statements are completely opposed to the solid doctrine handed down by tradition. "You believe in Christ born in the flesh," says St Augustine, "and you will come to Christ begotten of God."[148] In the Sacred Liturgy, the whole

---

[147] Col.3:1-2.
[148] Saint Augustine, *Enarr. in Ps.* 123, n. 2.

Christ is proposed to us in all the circumstances of His life, as the Word of the eternal Father, as born of the Virgin Mother of God, as He who teaches us truth, heals the sick, consoles the afflicted, who endures suffering and who dies; finally, as He who rose triumphantly from the dead and who, reigning in the glory of heaven, sends us the Holy Paraclete and who abides in His Church forever; "Jesus Christ, yesterday and today, and the same forever."[149] Besides, the liturgy shows us Christ not only as a model to be imitated but as a Master to whom we should listen readily, a Shepherd whom we should follow, Author of our salvation, the Source of our holiness and the Head of the Mystical Body whose members we are, living by His very life.

164. Since His bitter sufferings constitute the principal mystery of our redemption, it is only fitting that the Catholic faith should give it the greatest prominence. This mystery is the very centre of divine worship since the Mass represents and renews it every day and since all the sacraments are most closely united with the cross.[150]

165. Hence, the liturgical year, devotedly fostered and accompanied by the Church, is not a cold and lifeless representation of the events of the past, or a simple and bare record of a former age. It is rather Christ Himself who is ever living in His Church. Here He continues that journey of immense mercy which He lovingly began in His mortal life, going about doing good,[151] with the design of bringing men to know His mysteries and in a way live by them. These mysteries are ever present and active not in a vague and uncertain way as some modern writers hold, but in the way that Catholic doctrine teaches us. According to the Doctors of the Church, they are shining examples of Christian perfection, as well as sources of divine grace, due to the merit and prayers of Christ; they still influence us because each mystery brings its own special grace for our salvation. Moreover, our holy Mother the Church, while

---

[149] Heb. 13:8.
[150] Saint Thomas, *Summa Theologica* III^a, q. 49 and q. 62, art. 5.
[151] Cf. Acts, 10:38.

proposing for our contemplation the mysteries of our Redeemer, asks in her prayers for those gifts which would give her children the greatest possible share in the spirit of these mysteries through the merits of Christ. By means of His inspiration and help and through the co-operation of our wills we can receive from Him living vitality as branches do from the tree and members from the head; thus slowly and laboriously we can transform ourselves "unto the measure of the age of the fullness of Christ."[152]

III. The Feasts of the Saints

166. In the course of the liturgical year, besides the mysteries of Jesus Christ, the feasts of the saints are celebrated. Even though these feasts are of a lower and subordinate order, the Church always strives to put before the faithful examples of sanctity in order to move them to cultivate in themselves the virtues of the divine Redeemer.

167. We should imitate the virtues of the saints just as they imitated Christ, for in their virtues there shines forth under different aspects the splendour of Jesus Christ. Among some of these saints the zeal of the apostolate stood out, in others courage prevailed even to the shedding of blood, constant vigilance marked others out as they kept watch for the divine Redeemer, while in others the virginal purity of soul was resplendent and their modesty revealed the beauty of Christian humility; there burned in all of them the fire of charity towards God and their neighbour. The Sacred Liturgy puts all these gems of sanctity before us so that we may consider them for our salvation, and "rejoicing at their merits, we may be inflamed by their example."[153] It is necessary, then, to practice "in simplicity innocence, in charity concord, in humility modesty, diligence in government, readiness in helping those who labour, mercy in serving the poor, in defending truth, constancy, in the strict maintenance of discipline justice, so that nothing may be wanting

---

[152] Eph. 4:13.
[153] *Missale Romanum,* Collect for Third Mass of Several Martyrs outside Paschaltide.

in us of the virtues which have been proposed for our imitation. These are the footprints left by the saints in their journey homeward, that guided by them we might follow them into glory."[154] In order that we may be helped by our senses, also, the Church wishes that images of the saints be displayed in our churches, always, however, with the same intention "that we imitate the virtues of those whose images we venerate."[155]

168. But there is another reason why the Christian people should honour the saints in heaven, namely, to implore their help and "that we be aided by the pleadings of those whose praise is our delight."[156] Hence, it is easy to understand why the Sacred Liturgy provides us with many different prayers to invoke the intercession of the saints.

169. Among the saints in heaven the Virgin Mary Mother of God is venerated in a special way. Because of the mission she received from God, her life is most closely linked with the mysteries of Jesus Christ, and there is no one who has followed in the footsteps of the Incarnate Word more closely and with more merit than she: and no one has more grace and power over the most Sacred Heart of the Son of God and through Him with the Heavenly Father. Holier than the Cherubim and Seraphim, she enjoys unquestionably greater glory than all the other saints, for she is "full of grace,"[157] she is the Mother of God, who happily gave birth to the Redeemer for us. Since she is therefore, "Mother of mercy, our life, our sweetness and our hope," let us all cry to her "mourning and weeping in this vale of tears,"[158] and confidently place ourselves and all we have under her patronage. She became our Mother also when the divine Redeemer offered the sacrifice of Himself; and hence by this title also, we are her children. She teaches us all the virtues; she gives us her Son and

---

[154] Saint Bede the Venerable, *Hom. subd. 70* for Feast of All Saints.
[155] *Missale Romanum,* Collect for Mass of Saint John Damascene.
[156] Saint Bernard, *Sermon 2 for Feast of All Saints.*
[157] Luke, 1:28.
[158] "Salve Regina."

with Him all the help we need, for God "wished us to have everything through Mary."[159]

170. Throughout this liturgical journey which begins anew for us each year under the sanctifying action of the Church, and strengthened by the help and example of the saints, especially of the Immaculate Virgin Mary, "let us draw near with a true heart, in fullness of faith having our hearts sprinkled from an evil conscience, and our bodies washed with clean water,"[160] let us draw near to the "High Priest"[161] that with Him we may share His life and sentiments and by Him penetrate "even within the veil,"[162] and there honour the Heavenly Father for ever and ever.

171. Such is the nature and the object of the Sacred Liturgy: it treats of the Mass, the sacraments, the Divine Office; it aims at uniting our souls with Christ and sanctifying them through the divine Redeemer in order that Christ be honoured and, through Him and in Him, the most Holy Trinity, *Glory be to the Father, and to the Son, and to the Holy Ghost*.

---

[159] Saint Bernard, *In Nativ. B.M.V.*, 7.
[160] Heb. 10:22.
[161] Ibid., 10:21.
[162] Ibid., 6:19.

PART IV
PRACTICAL PASTORAL DIRECTIVES

I. Devotional Exercises are not to be Neglected

172. In order that the errors and inaccuracies, mentioned above, may be more easily removed from the Church, and that the faithful following safer norms may be able to use more fruitfully the liturgical apostolate, We have deemed it opportune, Venerable Brethren, to add some practical applications of the doctrine which We have explained.

173. When dealing with genuine and solid piety We stated that there could be no real opposition between the Sacred Liturgy and other religious practices, provided they be kept within legitimate bounds and performed for a legitimate purpose. In fact, there are certain exercises of piety which the Church recommends very much to clergy and religious.

174. It is Our wish also that the faithful, as well, should take part in these practices. The chief of these are: meditation on spiritual things, diligent examination of conscience, enclosed retreats, visits to the Blessed Sacrament, and those special prayers in honour of the Blessed Virgin Mary among which the rosary, as all know, has pride of place.[163]

175. From these multiple forms of piety, the inspiration and action of the Holy Spirit cannot be absent. Their purpose is, in various ways, to attract and direct our souls to God, purifying them from their sins, encouraging them to practice virtue and, finally, stimulating them to advance along the path of sincere piety by accustoming them to meditate on the eternal truths and disposing them better to contemplate the mysteries of the human and divine natures of Christ. Besides, since they develop a deeper spiritual life of the faithful, they prepare them to take part in

---

[163] Cf. Code of Canon Law, Can. 125.

sacred public functions with greater fruit, and they lessen the danger of liturgical prayers becoming an empty ritualism.

176. In keeping with your pastoral solicitude, Venerable Brethren, do not cease to recommend and encourage these exercises of piety from which the faithful, entrusted to your care, cannot but derive salutary fruit. Above all, do not allow - as some do, who are deceived under the pretext of restoring the liturgy or who idly claim that only liturgical rites are of any real value and dignity - that churches be closed during the hours not appointed for public functions, as has already happened in some places: where the adoration of the august sacrament and visits to our Lord in the tabernacles are neglected; where confession of devotion is discouraged; and devotion to the Virgin Mother of God, a sign of "predestination" according to the opinion of holy men, is so neglected, especially among the young, as to fade away and gradually vanish. Such conduct most harmful to Christian piety is like poisonous fruit, growing on the infected branches of a healthy tree, which must be cut off so that the life-giving sap of the tree may bring forth only the best fruit.

177. Since the opinions expressed by some about frequent confession are completely foreign to the spirit of Christ and His Immaculate Spouse and are also most dangerous to the spiritual life, let Us call to mind what with sorrow We wrote about this point in the encyclical on the Mystical Body. We urgently insist once more that what We expounded in very serious words be proposed by you for the serious consideration and dutiful obedience of your flock, especially to students for the priesthood and young clergy.

178. Take special care that as many as possible, not only of the clergy but of the laity and especially those in religious organisations and in the ranks of Catholic Action, take part in monthly days of recollection and in retreats of longer duration made with a view to growing in virtue. As We have previously stated, such spiritual exercises are most useful and even necessary to instil into souls solid virtue, and to strengthen them

in sanctity so as to be able to derive from the Sacred Liturgy more efficacious and abundant benefits.

179. As regards the different methods employed in these exercises, it is perfectly clear to all that in the Church on earth, no less than in the Church in heaven, there are many mansions,[164] and that asceticism cannot be the monopoly of anyone. It is the same spirit who breatheth where He will,[165] and who with differing gifts and in different ways enlightens and guides souls to sanctity. Let their freedom and the supernatural action of the Holy Spirit be so sacrosanct that no one presume to disturb or stifle them for any reason whatsoever.

180. However, it is well known that the spiritual exercises according to the method and norms of St Ignatius have been fully approved and earnestly recommended by Our predecessors on account of their admirable efficacy. We, too, for the same reason have approved and commended them and willingly do We repeat this now.

181. Any inspiration to follow and practice extraordinary exercises of piety must most certainly come from the Father of Lights, from whom every good and perfect gift descends;[166] and, of course, the criterion of this will be the effectiveness of these exercises in making the divine cult loved and spread daily ever more widely, and in making the faithful approach the sacraments with more longing desire, and in obtaining for all things holy due respect and honour. If on the contrary, they are an obstacle to principles and norms of divine worship, or if they oppose or hinder them, one must surely conclude that they are not in keeping with prudence and enlightened zeal.

182. There are, besides, other exercises of piety which, although not strictly belonging to the Sacred Liturgy, are, nevertheless, of special import and dignity, and may be considered in a certain

---

[164] Cf. John, 14:2.
[165] John, 3:8.
[166] Cf. James, 1:17.

way to be an addition to the liturgical cult; they have been approved and praised over and over again by the Apostolic See and by the bishops. Among these are the prayers usually said during the month of May in honour of the Blessed Virgin Mother of God, or during the month of June to the most Sacred Heart of Jesus: also novenas and triduums, stations of the cross and other similar practices.

183. These devotions make us partakers in a salutary manner of the liturgical cult, because they urge the faithful to go frequently to the sacrament of penance, to attend Mass and receive communion with devotion, and, as well, encourage them to meditate on the mysteries of our redemption and imitate the example of the saints.

184. Hence, he would do something very wrong and dangerous who would dare to take on himself to reform all these exercises of piety and reduce them completely to the methods and norms of liturgical rites. However, it is necessary that the spirit of the Sacred Liturgy and its directives should exercise such a salutary influence on them that nothing improper be introduced nor anything unworthy of the dignity of the house of God or detrimental to the sacred functions or opposed to solid piety.

185. Take care then, Venerable Brethren, that this true and solid piety increases daily more and more under your guidance and bears more abundant fruit. Above all, do not cease to inculcate into the minds of all that progress in the Christian life does not consist in the multiplicity and variety of prayers and exercises of piety, but rather in their helpfulness towards spiritual progress of the faithful and constant growth of the Church universal. For the eternal Father "chose us in Him [Christ] before the foundation of the world that we should be holy and unspotted in His sight."[167] All our prayers, then, and all our religious practices should aim at directing our spiritual energies towards attaining this most noble and lofty end.

---

[167] Eph. 1:4.

II. The Liturgical Spirit and Apostolate are be Promoted.

186. We earnestly exhort you, Venerable Brethren, that after errors and falsehoods have been removed, and anything that is contrary to truth or moderation has been condemned, you promote a deeper knowledge among the people of the Sacred Liturgy so that they more readily and easily follow the sacred rites and take part in them with true Christian dispositions.

187. First of all, you must strive that with due reverence and faith all obey the decrees of the Council of Trent, of the Roman Pontiffs, and the Sacred Congregation of Rites, and what the liturgical books ordain concerning external public worship.

188. Three characteristics of which Our predecessor Pius X spoke should adorn all liturgical services: sacredness, which abhors any profane influence; nobility, which true and genuine arts should serve and foster; and universality, which, while safeguarding local and legitimate custom, reveals the catholic unity of the Church.[168]

189. We desire to commend and urge the adornment of churches and altars. Let each one feel moved by the inspired word, "the zeal of thy house hath eaten me up;"[169] and strive as much as in him lies that everything in the church, including vestments and liturgical furnishings, even though not rich nor lavish, be perfectly clean and appropriate, since all is consecrated to the Divine Majesty. If We have previously disapproved of the error of those who would wish to outlaw images from churches on the plea of reviving an ancient tradition, We now deem it Our duty to censure the inconsiderate zeal of those who propose for veneration in the Churches and on the altars, without any just reason, a multitude of sacred images and statues, and also those who display unauthorised relics, those who emphasise special and insignificant practices, neglecting essential and necessary

---

[168] Cf. Apostolic Letter (Motu Proprio) *Tra le sollecitudini,* November 22, 1903.
[169] Ps. 68:9; John, 2:17.

things. They thus bring religion into derision and lessen the dignity of worship.

190. Let us recall, as well, the decree about "not introducing new forms of worship and devotion."[170] We commend the exact observance of this decree to your vigilance.

191. As regards music, let the clear and guiding norms of the Apostolic See be scrupulously observed. Gregorian chant, which the Roman Church considers her own as handed down from antiquity and kept under her close tutelage, is proposed to the faithful as belonging to them also. In certain parts of the liturgy the Church definitely prescribes it;[171] it makes the celebration of the sacred mysteries not only more dignified and solemn but helps very much to increase the faith and devotion of the congregation. For this reason, Our predecessors of immortal memory, Pius X and Pius XI, decree - and We are happy to confirm with Our authority the norms laid down by them - that in seminaries and religious institutes, Gregorian chant be diligently and zealously promoted, and moreover that the old *Scholæ Cantorum* be restored, at least in the principal churches. This has already been done with happy results in not a few places.[172]

192. Besides, "so that the faithful take a more active part in divine worship, let Gregorian chant be restored to popular use in the parts proper to the people. Indeed it is very necessary that the faithful attend the sacred ceremonies not as if they were outsiders or mute onlookers, but let them fully appreciate the beauty of the liturgy and take part in the sacred ceremonies, alternating their voices with the priest and the choir, according to the prescribed norms. If, please God, this is done, it will not happen that the congregation hardly ever or only in a low murmur answer the prayers in Latin or in the vernacular."[173] A congregation that is

---

[170] Supreme Sacred Congregation of the Holy Office, Decree of May 26, 1937.
[171] Cf. Pius X, Apostolic Letter (Motu Proprio) *Tra le sollecitudini.*
[172] Cf. Pius X, *loc. cit.*; Pius XI, Constitution *Divini cultus,* 2, 5.
[173] Pius XI, Constitution *Divini cultus,* 9.

devoutly present at the sacrifice, in which our Saviour together with His children redeemed with His sacred blood sings the nuptial hymn of His immense love, cannot keep silent, for "song befits the lover"[174] and, as the ancient saying has it, "he who sings well prays twice." Thus the Church militant, faithful as well as clergy, joins in the hymns of the Church triumphant and with the choirs of angels, and, all together, sing a wondrous and eternal hymn of praise to the most Holy Trinity in keeping with the words of the preface, "we pray thee, let our voices blend with theirs as we humbly praise thee."[175]

193. It cannot be said that modern music and singing should be entirely excluded from Catholic worship. For, if they are not profane nor unbecoming to the sacredness of the place and function, and do not spring from a desire of achieving extraordinary and unusual effects, then our churches must admit them since they can contribute in no small way to the splendour of the sacred ceremonies, can lift the mind to higher things and foster true devotion of soul.

194. We also exhort you, Venerable Brethren, to promote with care congregational singing, and to see to its accurate execution with all due dignity, since it easily stirs up and arouses the faith and piety of large gatherings of the faithful. Let the full harmonious singing of our people rise to heaven like the bursting of a thunderous sea[176] and let them testify by the melody of their song to the unity of their hearts and minds,[177] as becomes brothers and the children of the same Father.

195. What We have said about music, applies to the other fine arts, especially to architecture, sculpture and painting. Recent works of art which lend themselves to the materials of modern composition, should not be universally despised and rejected through prejudice. Modern art should be given free scope in the

---

[174] Saint Augustine, *Serm. 336*, n. 1.
[175] *Missale Romanum,* Preface.
[176] Saint Ambrose, *Hexameron*, 3:5, 23.
[177] Cf. Acts, 4:32.

due and reverent service of the Church and the sacred rites, provided that they preserve a correct balance between styles tending neither to extreme realism nor to excessive "symbolism," and that the needs of the Christian community are taken into consideration rather than the particular taste or talent of the individual artist. Thus modern art will be able to join its voice to that wonderful choir of praise to which have contributed, in honour of the Catholic faith, the greatest artists throughout the centuries. Nevertheless, in keeping with the duty of Our office, We cannot help deploring and condemning those works of art, recently introduced by some, which seem to be a distortion and perversion of true art and which at times openly shock Christian taste, modesty and devotion, and shamefully offend the true religious sense. These must be entirely excluded and banished from our churches, like "anything else that is not in keeping with the sanctity of the place."[178]

196. Keeping in mind, Venerable Brethren, pontifical norms and decrees, take great care to enlighten and direct the minds and hearts of the artists to whom is given the task today of restoring or rebuilding the many churches which have been ruined or completely destroyed by war. Let them be capable and willing to draw their inspiration from religion to express what is suitable and more in keeping with the requirements of worship. Thus the human arts will shine forth with a wondrous heavenly splendour, and contribute greatly to human civilisation, to the salvation of souls and the glory of God. The fine arts are really in conformity with religion when "as noblest handmaids they are at the service of divine worship."[179]

197. But there is something else of even greater importance, Venerable Brethren, which We commend to your apostolic zeal, in a very special manner. Whatever pertains to the external worship has assuredly its importance; however, the most pressing duty of Christians is to live the liturgical life, and increase and cherish its supernatural spirit.

---

[178] Code of Canon Law, can. 1178.
[179] Pius XI, Constitution *Divini cultus*.

198. Readily provide the young clerical student with facilities to understand the sacred ceremonies, to appreciate their majesty and beauty and to learn the rubrics with care, just as you do when he is trained in ascetics, in dogma and in canon law and pastoral theology. This should not be done merely for cultural reasons and to fit the student to perform religious rites in the future, correctly and with due dignity, but especially to lead him into closest union with Christ, the Priest, so that he may become a holy minister of sanctity.

199. Try in every way, with the means and helps that your prudence deems best, that the clergy and people become one in mind and heart, and that the Christian people take such an active part in the liturgy that it becomes a truly sacred action of due worship to the eternal Lord in which the priest, chiefly responsible for the souls of his parish, and the ordinary faithful are united together.

200. To attain this purpose, it will greatly help to select carefully good and upright young boys from all classes of citizens who will come generously and spontaneously to serve at the altar with careful zeal and exactness. Parents of higher social standing and culture should greatly esteem this office for their children. If these youths, under the watchful guidance of the priests, are properly trained and encouraged to fulfil the task committed to them punctually, reverently and constantly, then from their number will readily come fresh candidates for the priesthood. The clergy will not then complain - as, alas, sometimes happens even in Catholic places - that in the celebration of the august sacrifice they find no one to answer or serve them.

201. Above all, try with your constant zeal to have all the faithful attend the eucharistic sacrifice from which they may obtain abundant and salutary fruit; and carefully instruct them in all the legitimate ways We have described above so that they may devoutly participate in it. The Mass is the chief act of divine worship; it should also be the source and centre of Christian piety. Never think that you have satisfied your apostolic zeal

until you see your faithful approach in great numbers the celestial banquet which is a sacrament of devotion, a sign of unity and a bond of love.[180]

202. By means of suitable sermons and particularly by periodic conferences and lectures, by special study weeks and the like, teach the Christian people carefully about the treasures of piety contained in the Sacred Liturgy so that they may be able to profit more abundantly by these supernatural gifts. In this matter, those who are active in the ranks of Catholic Action will certainly be a help to you, since they are ever at the service of the hierarchy in the work of promoting the kingdom of Jesus Christ.

203. But in all these matters, it is essential that you watch vigilantly lest the enemy come into the field of the Lord and sow cockle among the wheat;[181] in other words, do not let your flocks be deceived by the subtle and dangerous errors of false mysticism or quietism - as you know We have already condemned these errors;[182] also do not let a certain dangerous "humanism" lead them astray, nor let there be introduced a false doctrine destroying the notion of Catholic faith, nor finally an exaggerated zeal for antiquity in matters liturgical. Watch with like diligence lest the false teaching of those be propagated who wrongly think and teach that the glorified human nature of Christ really and continually dwells in the "just" by His presence and that one and numerically the same grace, as they say, unites Christ with the members of His Mystical Body.

204. Never be discouraged by the difficulties that arise, and never let your pastoral zeal grow cold. "Blow the trumpet in Sion...call an assembly, gather together the people, sanctify the Church, assemble the ancients, gather together the little ones, and them that suck at the breasts,"[183] and use every help to get the faithful everywhere to fill the churches and crowd around the altars so

---

[180] Cf. Saint Augustine, *Tract. 26 in John 13.*
[181] Cf. Matt. 13:24-25.
[182] Encyclical letter *Mystici Corporis.*
[183] Joel, 2:15-16.

that they may be restored by the graces of the sacraments and joined as living members to their divine Head, and with Him and through Him celebrate together the august sacrifice that gives due tribute of praise to the Eternal Father.

EPILOGUE

205. These, Venerable Brethren, are the subjects We desired to write to you about. We are moved to write that your children, who are also Ours, may more fully understand and appreciate the most precious treasures which are contained in the Sacred Liturgy: namely, the eucharistic sacrifice, representing and renewing the sacrifice of the cross, the sacraments which are the streams of divine grace and of divine life, and the hymn of praise, which heaven and earth daily offer to God.

206. We cherish the hope that these Our exhortations will not only arouse the sluggish and recalcitrant to a deeper and more correct study of the liturgy, but also instil into their daily lives its supernatural spirit according to the words of the Apostle, "extinguish not the spirit."[184]

207. To those whom an excessive zeal occasionally led to say and do certain things which saddened Us and which We could not approve, We repeat the warning of St Paul, "But prove all things, hold fast that which is good."[185] Let Us paternally warn them to imitate in their thoughts and actions the Christian doctrine which is in harmony with the precepts of the immaculate Spouse of Jesus Christ, the mother of saints.

208. Let Us remind all that they must generously and faithfully obey their holy pastors who possess the right and duty of regulating the whole life, especially the spiritual life, of the Church. "Obey your prelates and be subject to them. For they watch as being to render an account of your souls; that they may do this with joy and not with grief."[186]

---

[184] I Thess. 5:19.
[185] Ibid., 5:21.
[186] Heb. 13:17

209. May God, whom we worship, and who is "not the God of dissension but of peace,"[187] graciously grant to us all that during our earthly exile we may with one mind and one heart participate in the Sacred Liturgy which is, as it were, a preparation and a token of that heavenly liturgy in which we hope one day to sing together with the most glorious Mother of God and our most loving Mother, "To Him that sitteth on the throne, and to the Lamb, benediction and honour, and glory and power for ever and ever."[188]

210. In this joyous hope, We most lovingly impart to each and every one of you, Venerable Brethren, and to the flocks confided to your care, as a pledge of divine gifts and as a witness of Our special love, the apostolic benediction.

Given at Castel Gandolfo, near Rome, on the 20th day of November in the year 1947, the 9th of Our Pontificate.

PIUS PP. XII

---

[187] 1 Cor.14:33.
[188] Apoc. 5:13.

SACROSANCTUM CONCILIUM

CONSTITUTION
ON THE SACRED LITURGY
OF THE SECOND VATICAN COUNCIL
SOLEMNLY PROMULGATED BY
HIS HOLINESS POPE PAUL VI
ON DECEMBER 4, 1963

INTRODUCTION

1. This Sacred Council has several aims in view: it desires to impart an ever increasing vigour to the Christian life of the faithful; to adapt more suitably to the needs of our own times those institutions which are subject to change; to foster whatever can promote union among all who believe in Christ; to strengthen whatever can help to call the whole of mankind into the household of the Church. The Council therefore sees particularly cogent reasons for undertaking the reform and promotion of the liturgy.

2. For the liturgy, "through which the work of our redemption is accomplished,"[1] most of all in the divine sacrifice of the eucharist, is the outstanding means whereby the faithful may express in their lives, and manifest to others, the mystery of Christ and the real nature of the true Church. It is of the essence of the Church that she be both human and divine, visible and yet invisibly equipped, eager to act and yet intent on contemplation, present in this world and yet not at home in it; and she is all these things in such wise that in her the human is directed and subordinated to the divine, the visible likewise to the invisible, action to contemplation, and this present world to that city yet to come,

---

[1] *Missale Romanum*, Secret of the ninth Sunday after Pentecost.

which we seek.[2] While the liturgy daily builds up those who are within into a holy temple of the Lord, into a dwelling place for God in the Spirit,[3] to the mature measure of the fullness of Christ,[4] at the same time it marvellously strengthens their power to preach Christ, and thus shows forth the Church to those who are outside as a sign lifted up among the nations[5] under which the scattered children of God may be gathered together,[6] until there is one sheepfold and one shepherd.[7]

3. Wherefore the Sacred Council judges that the following principles concerning the promotion and reform of the liturgy should be called to mind, and that practical norms should be established.

Among these principles and norms there are some which can and should be applied both to the Roman rite and also to all the other rites. The practical norms which follow, however, should be taken as applying only to the Roman rite, except for those which, in the very nature of things, affect other rites as well.

4. Lastly, in faithful obedience to tradition, the Sacred Council declares that holy Mother Church holds all lawfully acknowledged rites to be of equal right and dignity; that she wishes to preserve them in the future and to foster them in every way. The Council also desires that, where necessary, the rites be revised carefully in the light of sound tradition, and that they be given new vigour to meet the circumstances and needs of modern times.

---

[2] Cf. Heb. 13:14.
[3] Cf. Eph. 2:21-22.
[4] Cf. Eph. 4:13.
[5] Cf. Is. 11:12.
[6] Cf. John 11:52.
[7] Cf. John 10:16.

CHAPTER I
GENERAL PRINCIPLES FOR THE RESTORATION AND PROMOTION OF THE SACRED LITURGY

I. The Nature of the Sacred Liturgy and Its Importance in the Church's Life

5. God who "wills that all men be saved and come to the knowledge of the truth" (1 Tim. 2:4), "who in many and various ways spoke in times past to the fathers by the prophets" (Heb. 1:1), when the fullness of time had come sent His Son, the Word made flesh, anointed by the Holy Spirit, to preach the gospel to the poor, to heal the contrite of heart,[8] to be a "bodily and spiritual medicine,"[9] the Mediator between God and man.[10] For His humanity, united with the person of the Word, was the instrument of our salvation. Therefore in Christ "the perfect achievement of our reconciliation came forth, and the fullness of divine worship was given to us."[11]

The wonderful works of God among the people of the Old Testament were but a prelude to the work of Christ the Lord in redeeming mankind and giving perfect glory to God. He achieved His task principally by the Paschal Mystery of His blessed passion, resurrection from the dead, and the glorious ascension, whereby "dying, he destroyed our death and, rising, he restored our life."[12] For it was from the side of Christ as He slept the sleep of death upon the cross that there came forth "the wondrous sacrament of the whole Church."[13]

6. Just as Christ was sent by the Father, so also He sent the apostles, filled with the Holy Spirit. This He did that, by

---

[8] Cf. Is. 61:1; Luke 4:18.

[9] St Ignatius of Antioch, To the Ephesians, 7, 2.

[10] Cf. 1 Tim. 2:5.

[11] Sacramentarium Veronese (ed. Mohlberg), n. 1265; cf. also n. 1241, 1248.

[12] *Missale Romanum,* Easter Preface.

[13] Prayer before the third [not second] lesson for Holy Saturday, as it was in the Roman Missal before the [1955] restoration of Holy Week.

preaching the gospel to every creature,[14] they might proclaim that the Son of God, by His death and resurrection, had freed us from the power of Satan[15] and from death, and brought us into the kingdom of His Father. His purpose also was that they might accomplish the work of salvation which they had proclaimed, by means of sacrifice and sacraments, around which the entire liturgical life revolves. Thus by baptism men are plunged into the Paschal Mystery of Christ: they die with Him, are buried with Him, and rise with Him;[16] they receive the spirit of adoption as sons "in which we cry: Abba, Father" (Rom. 8:15), and thus become true adorers whom the Father seeks.[17] In like manner, as often as they eat the supper of the Lord they proclaim the death of the Lord until He comes.[18] For that reason, on the very day of Pentecost, when the Church appeared before the world, "those who received the word" of Peter "were baptised." And "they continued steadfastly in the teaching of the apostles and in the communion of the breaking of bread and in prayers...praising God and being in favour with all the people" (Acts 2:41-47). From that time onwards the Church has never failed to come together to celebrate the Paschal Mystery: reading those things "which were in all the scriptures concerning him" (Luke 24:27), celebrating the eucharist in which "the victory and triumph of his death are again made present,"[19] and at the same time giving thanks "to God for his unspeakable gift" (2 Cor. 9:15) in Christ Jesus, "in praise of his glory" (Eph. 1:12), through the power of the Holy Spirit.

7. To accomplish so great a work, Christ is always present in His Church, especially in her liturgical celebrations. He is present in the sacrifice of the Mass, not only in the person of His minister, "the same now offering, through the ministry of priests, who formerly offered himself on the cross,"[20] but especially under the

---

14 Cf. Mark 16:15.
15 Cf. Acts 26:18.
16 Cf. Rom. 6:4; Eph. 2:6; Col. 3:1; 2 Tim. 2:11.
17 Cf. John 4:23.
18 Cf. 1 Cor. 11:26.
19 Council of Trent, Session XIII, Decree on the Holy Eucharist, c.5.
20 Ibid., Session XXII, Doctrine on the Holy Sacrifice of the Mass, c. 2.

eucharistic species. By His power He is present in the sacraments, so that when a man baptises it is really Christ Himself who baptises.[21] He is present in His word, since it is He Himself who speaks when the holy scriptures are read in the Church. He is present, lastly, when the Church prays and sings, for He promised: "Where two or three are gathered together in my name, there am I in the midst of them" (Matt. 18:20) .

Christ indeed always associates the Church with Himself in this great work wherein God is perfectly glorified and men are sanctified. The Church is His beloved Bride who calls to her Lord, and through Him offers worship to the Eternal Father.

Rightly, then, the liturgy is considered as an exercise of the priestly office of Jesus Christ. In the liturgy the sanctification of man is signified by signs perceptible to the senses, and is effected in a way which corresponds with each of these signs; in the liturgy the whole public worship is performed by the Mystical Body of Jesus Christ, that is, by the Head and His members.

From this it follows that every liturgical celebration, because it is an action of Christ the priest and of His Body which is the Church, is a sacred action surpassing all others; no other action of the Church can equal its efficacy by the same title and to the same degree.

8. In the earthly liturgy we take part in a foretaste of that heavenly liturgy which is celebrated in the holy city of Jerusalem toward which we journey as pilgrims, where Christ is sitting at the right hand of God, a minister of the holies and of the true tabernacle;[22] we sing a hymn to the Lord's glory with all the warriors of the heavenly army; venerating the memory of the saints, we hope for some part and fellowship with them; we eagerly await the Saviour, Our Lord Jesus Christ, until He, our life, shall appear and we too will appear with Him in glory.[23]

---

[21] Cf. St Augustine, Tractatus in Ioannem, VI, n. 7.
[22] Cf. Apoc. 21:2; Col. 3:1; Heb. 8:2.
[23] Cf. Phil. 3:20; Col. 3:4.

9. The Sacred Liturgy does not exhaust the entire activity of the Church. Before men can come to the liturgy they must be called to faith and to conversion: "How then are they to call upon him in whom they have not yet believed? But how are they to believe him whom they have not heard? And how are they to hear if no one preaches? And how are men to preach unless they be sent?" (Rom. 10:14-15).

Therefore the Church announces the good tidings of salvation to those who do not believe, so that all men may know the true God and Jesus Christ whom He has sent, and may be converted from their ways, doing penance.[24] To believers also the Church must ever preach faith and penance, she must prepare them for the sacraments, teach them to observe all that Christ has commanded,[25] and invite them to all the works of charity, piety, and the apostolate. For all these works make it clear that Christ's faithful, though not of this world, are to be the light of the world and to glorify the Father before men.

10. Nevertheless the liturgy is the summit toward which the activity of the Church is directed; at the same time it is the font from which all her power flows. For the aim and object of apostolic works is that all who are made sons of God by faith and baptism should come together to praise God in the midst of His Church, to take part in the sacrifice, and to eat the Lord's supper.

The liturgy in its turn moves the faithful, filled with "the paschal sacraments," to be "one in holiness;"[26] it prays that "they may hold fast in their lives to what they have grasped by their faith;"[27] the renewal in the eucharist of the covenant between the Lord and man draws the faithful into the compelling love of Christ and sets them on fire. From the liturgy, therefore, and especially from the eucharist, as from a font, grace is poured forth upon us; and the sanctification of men in Christ and the glorification of God, to which all other activities of the Church are

---

[24] Cf. John 17:3; Luke 24:27; Acts 2:38.
[25] Cf. Matt. 28:20.
[26] *Missale Romanum,* Postcommunion for both Masses of Easter Sunday.
[27] Ibid., Collect of the Mass for Tuesday of Easter Week.

directed as toward their end, is achieved in the most efficacious possible way.

11. But in order that the liturgy may be able to produce its full effects, it is necessary that the faithful come to it with proper dispositions, that their minds should be attuned to their voices, and that they should co-operate with divine grace lest they receive it in vain.[28] Pastors of souls must therefore realise that, when the liturgy is celebrated, something more is required than the mere observation of the laws governing valid and licit celebration; it is their duty also to ensure that the faithful take part fully aware of what they are doing, actively engaged in the rite, and enriched by its effects.

12. The spiritual life, however, is not limited solely to participation in the liturgy. The Christian is indeed called to pray with his brethren, but he must also enter into his chamber to pray to the Father, in secret;[29] yet more, according to the teaching of the Apostle, he should pray without ceasing.[30] We learn from the same Apostle that we must always bear about in our body the dying of Jesus, so that the life also of Jesus may be made manifest in our bodily frame.[31] This is why we ask the Lord in the sacrifice of the Mass that, "receiving the offering of the spiritual victim," he may fashion us for himself "as an eternal gift."[32]

13. Popular devotions of the Christian people are to be highly commended, provided they accord with the laws and norms of the Church, above all when they are ordered by the Apostolic See.

Devotions proper to individual Churches also have a special dignity if they are undertaken by mandate of the bishops according to customs or books lawfully approved.

---

[28] Cf. 2 Cor. 6:1.
[29] Cf. Matt. 6:6.
[30] Cf . 1 Thess. 5:17.
[31] Cf . 2 Cor. 4:10-11.
[32] *Missale Romanum,* Secret for Monday of Pentecost Week.

But these devotions should be so drawn up that they harmonise with the liturgical seasons, accord with the Sacred Liturgy, are in some fashion derived from it, and lead the people to it, since, in fact, the liturgy by its very nature far surpasses any of them.

II. The Promotion of Liturgical Instruction and Active Participation

14. Mother Church earnestly desires that all the faithful should be led to that fully conscious, and active participation in liturgical celebrations which is demanded by the very nature of the liturgy. Such participation by the Christian people as "a chosen race, a royal priesthood, a holy nation, a redeemed people" (1 Pet. 2:9; cf. 2:4-5), is their right and duty by reason of their baptism.

In the restoration and promotion of the Sacred Liturgy, this full and active participation by all the people is the aim to be considered before all else; for it is the primary and indispensable source from which the faithful are to derive the true Christian spirit; and therefore pastors of souls must zealously strive to achieve it, by means of the necessary instruction, in all their pastoral work.

Yet it would be futile to entertain any hopes of realising this unless the pastors themselves, in the first place, become thoroughly imbued with the spirit and power of the liturgy, and undertake to give instruction about it. A prime need, therefore, is that attention be directed, first of all, to the liturgical instruction of the clergy. Wherefore the Sacred Council has decided to enact as follows:

15. Professors who are appointed to teach liturgy in seminaries, religious houses of study, and theological faculties must be properly trained for their work in institutes which specialise in this subject.

16. The study of Sacred Liturgy is to be ranked among the compulsory and major courses in seminaries and religious houses of studies; in theological faculties it is to rank among the principal courses. It is to be taught under its theological, historical,

spiritual, pastoral, and juridical aspects. Moreover, other professors, while striving to expound the mystery of Christ and the history of salvation from the angle proper to each of their own subjects, must nevertheless do so in a way which will clearly bring out the connection between their subjects and the liturgy, as also the unity which underlies all priestly training. This consideration is especially important for professors of dogmatic, spiritual, and pastoral theology and for those of holy scripture.

17. In seminaries and houses of religious, clerics shall be given a liturgical formation in their spiritual life. For this they will need proper direction, so that they may be able to understand the sacred rites and take part in them wholeheartedly; and they will also need personally to celebrate the sacred mysteries, as well as popular devotions which are imbued with the spirit of the liturgy. In addition they must learn how to observe the liturgical laws, so that life in seminaries and houses of religious may be thoroughly influenced by the spirit of the liturgy.

18. Priests, both secular and religious, who are already working in the Lord's vineyard are to be helped by every suitable means to understand ever more fully what it is that they are doing when they perform sacred rites; they are to be aided to live the liturgical life and to share it with the faithful entrusted to their care.

19. With zeal and patience, pastors of souls must promote the liturgical instruction of the faithful, and also their active participation in the liturgy both internally and externally, taking into account their age and condition, their way of life, and standard of religious culture. By so doing, pastors will be fulfilling one of the chief duties of a faithful dispenser of the mysteries of God; and in this matter they must lead their flock not only in word but also by example.

20. Transmissions of the sacred rites by radio and television shall be done with discretion and dignity, under the leadership and direction of a suitable person appointed for this office by the

bishops. This is especially important when the service to be broadcast is the Mass.

III. The Reform of the Sacred Liturgy

21. In order that the Christian people may more certainly derive an abundance of graces from the Sacred Liturgy, holy Mother Church desires to undertake with great care a general restoration of the liturgy itself. For the liturgy is made up of immutable elements divinely instituted, and of elements subject to change. These not only may but ought to be changed with the passage of time if they have suffered from the intrusion of anything out of harmony with the inner nature of the liturgy or have become unsuited to it.

In this restoration, both texts and rites should be drawn up so that they express more clearly the holy things which they signify; the Christian people, so far as possible, should be enabled to understand them with ease and to take part in them fully, actively, and as befits a community.

Wherefore the Sacred Council establishes the following general norms:

A) *General norms*

22.   § 1. Regulation of the Sacred Liturgy depends solely on the authority of the Church, that is, on the Apostolic See and, as laws may determine, on the bishop.

§ 2. In virtue of power conceded by the law, the regulation of the liturgy within certain defined limits belongs also to various kinds of competent territorial bodies of bishops legitimately established.

§ 3. Therefore no other person, even if he be a priest, may add, remove, or change anything in the liturgy on his own authority.

23. That sound tradition may be retained, and yet the way remain open to legitimate progress, careful investigation is always to be made into each part of the liturgy which is to be revised. This investigation should be theological, historical, and pastoral. Also

the general laws governing the structure and meaning of the liturgy must be studied in conjunction with the experience derived from recent liturgical reforms and from the indults conceded to various places. Finally, there must be no innovations unless the good of the Church genuinely and certainly requires them; and care must be taken that any new forms adopted should in some way grow organically from forms already existing.

As far as possible, notable differences between the rites used in adjacent regions must be carefully avoided.

24. Sacred scripture is of the greatest importance in the celebration of the liturgy. For it is from scripture that lessons are read and explained in the homily, and psalms are sung; the prayers, collects, and liturgical songs are scriptural in their inspiration and their force, and it is from the scriptures that actions and signs derive their meaning. Thus to achieve the restoration, progress, and adaptation of the Sacred Liturgy, it is essential to promote that warm and living love for scripture to which the venerable tradition of both eastern and western rites gives testimony.

25. The liturgical books are to be revised as soon as possible; experts are to be employed on the task, and bishops are to be consulted, from various parts of the world.

B) Norms drawn from the hierarchic and communal nature of the Liturgy

26. Liturgical services are not private functions, but are celebrations of the Church, which is the "sacrament of unity," namely, the holy people united and ordered under their bishops.[33]

Therefore liturgical services pertain to the whole body of the Church; they manifest it and have effects upon it; but they concern the individual members of the Church in different ways, according to their differing rank, office, and actual participation.

---

[33] St Cyprian, *On the Unity of the Catholic Church*, 7; cf. Letter 66, n. 8, 3.

27. It is to be stressed that whenever rites, according to their specific nature, make provision for communal celebration involving the presence and active participation of the faithful, this way of celebrating them is to be preferred, so far as possible, to a celebration that is individual and quasi-private.

This applies with especial force to the celebration of Mass and the administration of the sacraments, even though every Mass has of itself a public and social nature.

28. In liturgical celebrations each person, minister or layman, who has an office to perform, should do all of, but only, those parts which pertain to his office by the nature of the rite and the principles of liturgy.

29. Servers, lectors, commentators, and members of the choir also exercise a genuine liturgical function. They ought, therefore, to discharge their office with the sincere piety and decorum demanded by so exalted a ministry and rightly expected of them by God's people.

Consequently they must all be deeply imbued with the spirit of the liturgy, each in his own measure, and they must be trained to perform their functions in a correct and orderly manner.

30. To promote active participation, the people should be encouraged to take part by means of acclamations, responses, psalmody, antiphons, and songs, as well as by actions, gestures and bodily attitudes. And at the proper times all should observe a reverent silence.

31. The revision of the liturgical books must carefully attend to the provision of rubrics also for the people's parts.

32. The liturgy makes distinctions between persons according to their liturgical function and Sacred Orders, and there are liturgical laws providing for due honours to be given to civil authorities. Apart from these instances, no special honours are to be paid in the liturgy to any private persons or classes of persons, whether in the ceremonies or by external display.

C) Norms based upon the didactic and pastoral nature of the Liturgy

33. Although the Sacred Liturgy is above all things the worship of the divine Majesty, it likewise contains much instruction for the faithful.[34] For in the liturgy God speaks to His people and Christ is still proclaiming His gospel. And the people reply to God both by song and prayer.

Moreover, the prayers addressed to God by the priest who presides over the assembly in the person of Christ are said in the name of the entire holy people and of all present. And the visible signs used by the liturgy to signify invisible divine things have been chosen by Christ or the Church. Thus not only when things are read "which were written for our instruction" (Rom. 15:4), but also when the Church prays or sings or acts, the faith of those taking part is nourished and their minds are raised to God, so that they may offer Him their rational service and more abundantly receive His grace.

Wherefore, in the revision of the liturgy, the following general norms should be observed:

34. The rites should be distinguished by a noble simplicity; they should be short, clear, and unencumbered by useless repetitions; they should be within the people's powers of comprehension, and normally should not require much explanation.

35. That the intimate connection between words and rites may be apparent in the liturgy:
1) In sacred celebrations there is to be more reading from holy scripture, and it is to be more varied and suitable.
2) Because the sermon is part of the liturgical service, the best place for it is to be indicated even in the rubrics, as far as the nature of the rite will allow; the ministry of preaching is to be fulfilled with exactitude and fidelity. The sermon, moreover, should draw its content mainly from scriptural and liturgical

---

[34] Cf. Council of Trent, Session XXII, Doctrine on the Holy Sacrifice of the Mass, c. 8.

sources, and its character should be that of a proclamation of God's wonderful works in the history of salvation, the mystery of Christ, ever made present and active within us, especially in the celebration of the liturgy.

3) Instruction which is more explicitly liturgical should also be given in a variety of ways; if necessary, short directives to be spoken by the priest or proper minister should be provided within the rites themselves. But they should occur only at the more suitable moments, and be in prescribed or similar words.

4) Bible services should be encouraged, especially on the vigils of the more solemn feasts, on some weekdays in Advent and Lent, and on Sundays and feast days. They are particularly to be commended in places where no priest is available; when this is so, a deacon or some other person authorised by the bishop should preside over the celebration.

36. § 1. Particular law remaining in force, the use of the Latin language is to be preserved in the Latin rites.

§ 2. But since the use of the mother tongue, whether in the Mass, the administration of the sacraments, or other parts of the liturgy, frequently may be of great advantage to the people, the limits of its employment may be extended. This will apply in the first place to the readings and directives, and to some of the prayers and chants, according to the regulations on this matter to be laid down separately in subsequent chapters.

§ 3. These norms being observed, it is for the competent territorial ecclesiastical authority mentioned in Art. 22, 2, to decide whether, and to what extent, the vernacular language is to be used; their decrees are to be approved, that is, confirmed, by the Apostolic See. And, whenever it seems to be called for, this authority is to consult with bishops of neighbouring regions which have the same language.

§ 4. Translations from the Latin text into the mother tongue intended for use in the liturgy must be approved by the competent territorial ecclesiastical authority mentioned above.

D) *Norms for adapting the Liturgy to the culture and traditions of peoples*

37. Even in the liturgy, the Church has no wish to impose a rigid uniformity in matters which do not implicate the faith or the good of the whole community; rather does she respect and foster the genius and talents of the various races and peoples. Anything in these peoples' way of life which is not indissolubly bound up with superstition and error she studies with sympathy and, if possible, preserves intact. Sometimes in fact she admits such things into the liturgy itself, so long as they harmonise with its true and authentic spirit.

38. Provisions shall also be made, when revising the liturgical books, for legitimate variations and adaptations to different groups, regions, and peoples, especially in mission lands, provided that the substantial unity of the Roman rite is preserved; and this should be borne in mind when drawing up the rites and devising rubrics.

39. Within the limits set by the typical editions of the liturgical books, it shall be for the competent territorial ecclesiastical authority mentioned in Art. 22, 2, to specify adaptations, especially in the case of the administration of the sacraments, the sacramentals, processions, liturgical language, sacred music, and the arts, but according to the fundamental norms laid down in this Constitution.

40. In some places and circumstances, however, an even more radical adaptation of the liturgy is needed, and this entails greater difficulties. Wherefore:
1) The competent territorial ecclesiastical authority mentioned in Art. 22, 2, must, in this matter, carefully and prudently consider which elements from the traditions and culture of individual peoples might appropriately be admitted into divine worship. Adaptations which are judged to be useful or necessary should then be submitted to the Apostolic See, by whose consent they may be introduced.

2) To ensure that adaptations may be made with all the circumspection which they demand, the Apostolic See will grant power to this same territorial ecclesiastical authority to permit and to direct, as the case requires, the necessary preliminary experiments over a determined period of time among certain groups suited for the purpose.

3) Because liturgical laws often involve special difficulties with respect to adaptation, particularly in mission lands, men who are experts in these matters must be employed to formulate them.

E) Promotion of Liturgical Life in Diocese and Parish

41. The bishop is to be considered as the high priest of his flock, from whom the life in Christ of his faithful is in some way derived and dependent.

Therefore all should hold in great esteem the liturgical life of the diocese centred around the bishop, especially in his cathedral church; they must be convinced that the pre-eminent manifestation of the Church consists in the full active participation of all God's holy people in these liturgical celebrations, especially in the same eucharist, in a single prayer, at one altar, at which there presides the bishop surrounded by his college of priests and by his ministers.[35]

42. But because it is impossible for the bishop always and everywhere to preside over the whole flock in his Church, he cannot do other than establish lesser groupings of the faithful. Among these the parishes, set up locally under a pastor who takes the place of the bishop, are the most important: for in some manner they represent the visible Church constituted throughout the world.

And therefore the liturgical life of the parish and its relationship to the bishop must be fostered theoretically and practically among the faithful and clergy; efforts also must be made to encourage a sense of community within the parish, above all in the common celebration of the Sunday Mass.

---

[35] Cf. St Ignatius of Antioch, to the Smyrnians, 8; to the Magnesians, 7; to the Philadelphians, 4.

F) *The Promotion of Pastoral-Liturgical Action*

43. Zeal for the promotion and restoration of the liturgy is rightly held to be a sign of the providential dispositions of God in our time, as a movement of the Holy Spirit in His Church. It is today a distinguishing mark of the Church's life, indeed of the whole tenor of contemporary religious thought and action.

So that this pastoral-liturgical action may become even more vigorous in the Church, the Sacred Council decrees:

44. It is desirable that the competent territorial ecclesiastical authority mentioned in Art. 22, 2, set up a liturgical commission, to be assisted by experts in liturgical science, sacred music, art and pastoral practice. So far as possible the commission should be aided by some kind of Institute for Pastoral Liturgy, consisting of persons who are eminent in these matters, and including laymen as circumstances suggest. Under the direction of the above-mentioned territorial ecclesiastical authority the commission is to regulate pastoral-liturgical action throughout the territory, and to promote studies and necessary experiments whenever there is question of adaptations to be proposed to the Apostolic See.

45. For the same reason every diocese is to have a commission on the Sacred Liturgy under the direction of the bishop, for promoting the liturgical apostolate.

Sometimes it may be expedient that several dioceses should form between them one single commission which will be able to promote the liturgy by common consultation.

46. Besides the commission on the Sacred Liturgy, every diocese, as far as possible, should have commissions for sacred music and sacred art.

These three commissions must work in closest collaboration; indeed it will often be best to fuse the three of them into one single commission.

CHAPTER II
THE MOST SACRED MYSTERY OF THE EUCHARIST

47. At the Last Supper, on the night when He was betrayed, our Saviour instituted the eucharistic sacrifice of His Body and Blood. He did this in order to perpetuate the sacrifice of the Cross throughout the centuries until He should come again, and so to entrust to His beloved spouse, the Church, a memorial of His death and resurrection: a sacrament of love, a sign of unity, a bond of charity,[36] a paschal banquet in which Christ is eaten, the mind is filled with grace, and a pledge of future glory is given to us.[37]

48. The Church, therefore, earnestly desires that Christ's faithful, when present at this mystery of faith, should not be there as strangers or silent spectators; on the contrary, through a good understanding of the rites and prayers they should take part in the sacred action conscious of what they are doing, with devotion and full collaboration. They should be instructed by God's word and be nourished at the table of the Lord's body; they should give thanks to God; by offering the Immaculate Victim, not only through the hands of the priest, but also with him, they should learn also to offer themselves; through Christ the Mediator,[38] they should be drawn day by day into ever more perfect union with God and with each other, so that finally God may be all in all.

49. For this reason the Sacred Council, having in mind those Masses which are celebrated with the assistance of the faithful, especially on Sundays and feasts of obligation, has made the following decrees in order that the sacrifice of the Mass, even in

---

[36] Cf. St Augustine, Tractatus in Ioannem, VI, n. 13.
[37] *Breviarium Romanum,* feast of Corpus Christi, Second Vespers, antiphon to the Magnificat.
[38] Cf. St Cyril of Alexandria, Commentary on the Gospel of John, book XI, chap. XI-XII: Migne, Patrologia Graeca, 74, 557-564.

the ritual forms of its celebration, may become pastorally efficacious to the fullest degree.

50. The rite of the Mass is to be revised in such a way that the intrinsic nature and purpose of its several parts, as also the connection between them, may be more clearly manifested, and that devout and active participation by the faithful may be more easily achieved.

For this purpose the rites are to be simplified, due care being taken to preserve their substance; elements which, with the passage of time, came to be duplicated, or were added with but little advantage, are now to be discarded; other elements which have suffered injury through accidents of history are now to be restored to the vigour which they had in the days of the holy Fathers, as may seem useful or necessary.

51. The treasures of the bible are to be opened up more lavishly, so that richer fare may be provided for the faithful at the table of God's word. In this way a more representative portion of the holy scriptures will be read to the people in the course of a prescribed number of years.

52. By means of the homily the mysteries of the faith and the guiding principles of the Christian life are expounded from the sacred text, during the course of the liturgical year; the homily, therefore, is to be highly esteemed as part of the liturgy itself; in fact, at those Masses which are celebrated with the assistance of the people on Sundays and feasts of obligation, it should not be omitted except for a serious reason.

53. Especially on Sundays and feasts of obligation there is to be restored, after the Gospel and the homily, "the common prayer" or "the prayer of the faithful." By this prayer, in which the people are to take part, intercession will be made for holy Church, for the civil authorities, for those oppressed by various needs, for all mankind, and for the salvation of the entire world.[39]

---

[39] Cf. 1 Tim. 2:1-2.

54. In Masses which are celebrated with the people, a suitable place may be allotted to their mother tongue. This is to apply in the first place to the readings and "the common prayer," but also, as local conditions may warrant, to those parts which pertain to the people, according to the norms laid down in Art. 36 of this Constitution.

Nevertheless steps should be taken so that the faithful may also be able to say or to sing together in Latin those parts of the Ordinary of the Mass which pertain to them.

And wherever a more extended use of the mother tongue within the Mass appears desirable, the regulation laid down in Art. 40 of this Constitution is to be observed.

55. That more perfect form of participation in the Mass whereby the faithful, after the priest's communion, receive the Lord's body from the same sacrifice, is strongly commended.

The dogmatic principles which were laid down by the Council of Trent remaining intact,[40] communion under both kinds may be granted when the bishops think fit, not only to clerics and religious, but also to the laity, in cases to be determined by the Apostolic See, as, for instance, to the newly ordained in the Mass of their sacred ordination, to the newly professed in the Mass of their religious profession, and to the newly baptised in the Mass which follows their baptism.

56. The two parts which, in a certain sense, go to make up the Mass, namely, the liturgy of the word and the eucharistic liturgy, are so closely connected with each other that they form but one single act of worship. Accordingly this Sacred Synod strongly urges pastors of souls that, when instructing the faithful, they insistently teach them to take their part in the entire Mass, especially on Sundays and feasts of obligation.

---

[40] Session XXI, July 16, 1562. Doctrine on Communion under Both Species, chap. 1-3: Concilium Tridentinum. Diariorum, Actorum, Epistolarum, Tractatuum nova collectio ed. Soc. Goerresiana, tome VIII (Freiburg in Br., 1919), 698-699.

57.§1. Concelebration, whereby the unity of the priesthood is appropriately manifested, has remained in use to this day in the Church both in the east and in the west. For this reason it has seemed good to the Council to extend permission for concelebration to the following cases:

1.   a) on the Thursday of the Lord's Supper, not only at the Mass of the Chrism, but also at the evening Mass.

         b) at Masses during councils, bishops' conferences, and synods;

         c) at the Mass for the blessing of an abbot.

2. Also, with permission of the ordinary, to whom it belongs to decide whether concelebration is opportune:

         a) at conventual Mass, and at the principle Mass in churches when the needs of the faithful do not require that all priests available should celebrate individually;

         b) at Masses celebrated at any kind of priests' meetings, whether the priests be secular clergy or religious.

§2. 1. The regulation, however, of the discipline of concelebration in the diocese pertains to the bishop.

2. Nevertheless, each priest shall always retain his right to celebrate Mass individually, though not at the same time in the same church as a concelebrated Mass, nor on Thursday of the Lord's Supper.

58. A new rite for concelebration is to be drawn up and inserted into the Pontifical and into the Roman Missal.

CHAPTER III
THE OTHER SACRAMENTS
AND THE SACRAMENTALS

59. The purpose of the sacraments is to sanctify men, to build up the body of Christ, and, finally, to give worship to God; because they are signs they also instruct. They not only presuppose faith, but by words and objects they also nourish, strengthen, and express it; that is why they are called "sacraments of faith." They do indeed impart grace, but, in addition, the very act of celebrating them most effectively disposes the faithful to receive this grace in a fruitful manner, to worship God duly, and to practice charity.

It is therefore of the highest importance that the faithful should easily understand the sacramental signs, and should frequent with great eagerness those sacraments which were instituted to nourish the Christian life.

60. Holy Mother Church has, moreover, instituted sacramentals. These are sacred signs which bear a resemblance to the sacraments: they signify effects, particularly of a spiritual kind, which are obtained through the Church's intercession. By them men are disposed to receive the chief effect of the sacraments, and various occasions in life are rendered holy.

61. Thus, for well-disposed members of the faithful, the liturgy of the sacraments and sacramentals sanctifies almost every event in their lives; they are given access to the stream of divine grace which flows from the Paschal Mystery of the passion, death, the resurrection of Christ, the font from which all sacraments and sacramentals draw their power. There is hardly any proper use of material things which cannot thus be directed toward the sanctification of men and the praise of God.

62. With the passage of time, however, there have crept into the rites of the sacraments and sacramentals certain features which have rendered their nature and purpose far from clear to the

people of today; hence some changes have become necessary to adapt them to the needs of our own times. For this reason the Sacred Council decrees as follows concerning their revision.

63. Because the use of the mother tongue in the administration of the sacraments and sacramentals can often be of considerable help to the people, this use is to be extended according to the following norms:

a) The vernacular language may be used in administering the sacraments and sacramentals, according to the norm of Art. 36.

b) In harmony with the new edition of the Roman Ritual, particular rituals shall be prepared without delay by the competent territorial ecclesiastical authority mentioned in Art. 22, 2, of this Constitution. These rituals, which are to be adapted, also as regards the language employed, to the needs of the different regions, are to be reviewed by the Apostolic See and then introduced into the regions for which they have been prepared. But in drawing up these rituals or particular collections of rites, the instructions prefixed to the individual rites of the Roman Ritual, whether they be pastoral and rubrical or whether they have special social import, shall not be omitted.

64. The catechumenate for adults, comprising several distinct steps, is to be restored and to be taken into use at the discretion of the local ordinary. By this means the time of the catechumenate, which is intended as a period of suitable instruction, may be sanctified by sacred rites to be celebrated at successive intervals of time.

65. In mission lands it is found that some of the peoples already make use of initiation rites. Elements from these, when capable of being adapted to Christian ritual, may be admitted along with those already found in Christian tradition, according to the norm laid down in Art. 37-40, of this Constitution.

66. Both the rites for the baptism of adults are to be revised: not only the simpler rite, but also the more solemn one, which must take into account the restored catechumenate. A special Mass "for the conferring of baptism" is to be inserted into the Roman Missal.

67. The rite for the baptism of infants is to be revised, and it should be adapted to the circumstance that those to be baptised are, in fact, infants. The roles of parents and godparents, and also their duties, should be brought out more clearly in the rite itself.

68. The baptismal rite should contain variants, to be used at the discretion of the local ordinary, for occasions when a very large number are to be baptised together. Moreover, a shorter rite is to be drawn up, especially for mission lands, to be used by catechists, but also by the faithful in general when there is danger of death, and neither priest nor deacon is available.

69. In place of the rite called the "Order of supplying what was omitted in the baptism of an infant," a new rite is to be drawn up. This should manifest more fittingly and clearly that the infant, baptised by the short rite, has already been received into the Church.

And a new rite is to be drawn up for converts who have already been validly baptised; it should indicate that they are now admitted to communion with the Church.

70. Except during Eastertide, baptismal water may be blessed within the rite of baptism itself by an approved shorter formula.

71. The rite of confirmation is to be revised and the intimate connection which this sacrament has with the whole of Christian initiation is to be more clearly set forth; for this reason it is fitting for candidates to renew their baptismal promises just before they are confirmed.

Confirmation may be given within the Mass when convenient; when it is given outside the Mass, the rite that is used should be introduced by a formula to be drawn up for this purpose.

72. The rite and formulas for the sacrament of penance are to be revised so that they more clearly express both the nature and effect of the sacrament.

73. "Extreme unction," which may also and more fittingly be called "anointing of the sick," is not a sacrament for those only who are at the point of death. Hence, as soon as any one of the faithful begins to be in danger of death from sickness or old age, the fitting time for him to receive this sacrament has certainly already arrived.

74. In addition to the separate rites for anointing of the sick and for viaticum, a continuous rite shall be prepared according to which the sick man is anointed after he has made his confession and before he receives viaticum.

75. The number of the anointings is to be adapted to the occasion, and the prayers which belong to the rite of anointing are to be revised so as to correspond with the varying conditions of the sick who receive the sacrament.

76. Both the ceremonies and texts of the ordination rites are to be revised. The address given by the bishop at the beginning of each ordination or consecration may be in the mother tongue.

When a bishop is consecrated, the laying of hands may be done by all the bishops present.

77. The marriage rite now found in the Roman Ritual is to be revised and enriched in such a way that the grace of the sacrament is more clearly signified and the duties of the spouses are taught.

"If any regions are wont to use other praiseworthy customs and ceremonies when celebrating the sacrament of matrimony, the Sacred Synod earnestly desires that these by all means be retained."[41]

---

[41] Council of Trent, Session XXIV, November 11, 1563, On Reform, chap. I. Cf. Roman Ritual, title VIII, chap. II, n. 6.

Moreover the competent territorial ecclesiastical authority mentioned in Art. 22, 2 of this Constitution is free to draw up its own rite suited to the usages of place and people, according to the provision of Art. 63. But the rite must always conform to the law that the priest assisting at the marriage must ask for and obtain the consent of the contracting parties.

78. Matrimony is normally to be celebrated within the Mass, after the reading of the gospel and the homily, and before "the prayer of the faithful." The prayer for the bride, duly amended to remind both spouses of their equal obligation to remain faithful to each other, may be said in the mother tongue.

But if the sacrament of matrimony is celebrated apart from Mass, the epistle and gospel from the nuptial Mass are to be read at the beginning of the rite, and the blessing should always be given to the spouses.

79. The sacramentals are to undergo a revision which takes into account the primary principle of enabling the faithful to participate intelligently, actively, and easily; the circumstances of our own days must also be considered. When rituals are revised, as laid down in Art. 63, new sacramentals may also be added as the need for these becomes apparent.

Reserved blessings shall be very few; reservations shall be in favour of bishops or ordinaries.

Let provision be made that some sacramentals, at least in special circumstances and at the discretion of the ordinary, may be administered by qualified lay persons.

80. The rite for the consecration of virgins at present found in the Roman Pontifical is to be revised.

Moreover, a rite of religious profession and renewal of vows shall be drawn up in order to achieve greater unity, sobriety, and dignity. Apart from exceptions in particular law, this rite should be adopted by those who make their profession or renewal of vows within the Mass.

Religious profession should preferably be made within the Mass.

81. The rite for the burial of the dead should express more clearly the paschal character of Christian death, and should correspond more closely to the circumstances and traditions found in various regions. This holds good also for the liturgical colour to be used.

82. The rite for the burial of infants is to be revised, and a special Mass for the occasion should be provided.

CHAPTER IV
THE DIVINE OFFICE

83. Christ Jesus, high priest of the new and eternal covenant, taking human nature, introduced into this earthly exile that hymn which is sung throughout all ages in the halls of heaven. He joins the entire community of mankind to Himself, associating it with His own singing of this canticle of divine praise.

For he continues His priestly work through the agency of His Church, which is ceaselessly engaged in praising the Lord and interceding for the salvation of the whole world. She does this, not only by celebrating the eucharist, but also in other ways, especially by praying the Divine Office.

84. By tradition going back to early Christian times, the Divine Office is devised so that the whole course of the day and night is made holy by the praises of God. Therefore, when this wonderful song of praise is rightly performed by priests and others who are deputed for this purpose by the Church's ordinance, or by the faithful praying together with the priest in the approved form, then it is truly the voice of the bride addressed to her bridegroom; it is the very prayer which Christ Himself, together with His body, addresses to the Father.

85. Hence all who render this service are not only fulfilling a duty of the Church, but also are sharing in the greatest honour of Christ's spouse, for by offering these praises to God they are standing before God's throne in the name of the Church their Mother.

86. Priests who are engaged in the sacred pastoral ministry will offer the praises of the hours with greater fervour the more vividly they realise that they must heed St Paul's exhortation: "Pray without ceasing" (1 Thess. 5:11). For the work in which they labour will effect nothing and bring forth no fruit except by the power of the Lord who said: "Without me you can do nothing" (John 15: 5). That is why the apostles, instituting

deacons, said: "We will devote ourselves to prayer and to the ministry of the word" (Acts 6:4).

87. In order that the Divine Office may be better and more perfectly prayed in existing circumstances, whether by priests or by other members of the Church, the Sacred Council, carrying further the restoration already so happily begun by the Apostolic See, has seen fit to decree as follows concerning the office of the Roman rite.

88. Because the purpose of the office is to sanctify the day, the traditional sequence of the hours is to be restored so that once again they may be genuinely related to the time of the day when they are prayed, as far as this may be possible. Moreover, it will be necessary to take into account the modern conditions in which daily life has to be lived, especially by those who are called to labour in apostolic works.

89. Therefore, when the office is revised, these norms are to be observed:

   a) By the venerable tradition of the universal Church, Lauds as morning prayer and Vespers as evening prayer are the two hinges on which the daily office turns; hence they are to be considered as the chief hours and are to be celebrated as such.
   b) Compline is to be drawn up so that it will be a suitable prayer for the end of the day.
   c) The hour known as Matins, although it should retain the character of nocturnal praise when celebrated in choir, shall be adapted so that it may be recited at any hour of the day; it shall be made up of fewer psalms and longer readings.
   d) The hour of Prime is to be suppressed.
   e) In choir the hours of Terce, Sext, and None are to be observed. But outside choir it will be lawful to select any one of these three, according to the respective time of the day.

90. The Divine Office, because it is the public prayer of the Church, is a source of piety, and nourishment for personal prayer. And therefore priests and all others who take part in the Divine Office are earnestly exhorted in the Lord to attune their minds to their voices when praying it. The better to achieve this, let them take steps to improve their understanding of the liturgy and of the bible, especially of the psalms.

In revising the Roman office, its ancient and venerable treasures are to be so adapted that all those to whom they are handed on may more extensively and easily draw profit from them.

91. So that it may really be possible in practice to observe the course of the hours proposed in Art. 89, the psalms are no longer to be distributed throughout one week, but through some longer period of time.

The work of revising the psalter, already happily begun, is to be finished as soon as possible, and is to take into account the style of Christian Latin, the liturgical use of psalms, also when sung, and the entire tradition of the Latin Church.

92. As regards the readings, the following shall be observed:
   a) Readings from sacred scripture shall be arranged so that the riches of God's word may be easily accessible in more abundant measure.
   b) Readings excerpted from the works of the Fathers, Doctors, and ecclesiastical writers shall be better selected.
   c) The accounts of martyrdom or the lives of the saints are to accord with the facts of history.

93. To whatever extent may seem desirable, the hymns are to be restored to their original form, and whatever smacks of mythology or ill accords with Christian piety is to be removed or changed. Also, as occasion may arise, let other selections from the treasury of hymns be incorporated.

94. That the day may be truly sanctified, and that the hours themselves may be recited with spiritual advantage, it is best that

each of them be prayed at a time which most closely corresponds with its true canonical time.

95. Communities obliged to choral office are bound to celebrate the office in choir every day in addition to the conventual Mass. In particular:

    a) Orders of canons, of monks and of nuns, and of other regulars bound by law or constitutions to choral office must celebrate the entire office.

    b) Cathedral or collegiate chapters are bound to recite those parts of the office imposed on them by general or particular law.

    c) All members of the above communities who are in major orders or who are solemnly professed, except for lay brothers, are bound to recite individually those canonical hours which they do not pray in choir.

96. Clerics not bound to office in choir, if they are in major orders, are bound to pray the entire office every day, either in common or individually, as laid down in Art. 89.

97. Appropriate instances are to be defined by the rubrics in which a liturgical service may be substituted for the Divine Office.

    In particular cases, and for a just reason, ordinaries can dispense their subjects wholly or in part from the obligation of reciting the Divine Office, or may commute the obligation.

98. Members of any institute dedicated to acquiring perfection who, according to their constitutions, are to recite any parts of the Divine Office are thereby performing the public prayer of the Church.

    They too perform the public prayer of the Church who, in virtue of their constitutions, recite any short office, provided this is drawn up after the pattern of the Divine Office and is duly approved.

99. Since the Divine Office is the voice of the Church, that is of the whole mystical body publicly praising God, those clerics who are

not obliged to office in choir, especially priests who live together or who assemble for any purpose, are urged to pray at least some part of the Divine Office in common.

All who pray the Divine Office, whether in choir or in common, should fulfil the task entrusted to them as perfectly as possible: this refers not only to the internal devotion of their minds but also to their external manner of celebration.

It is, moreover, fitting that the office, both in choir and in common, be sung when possible.

100. Pastors of souls should see to it that the chief hours, especially Vespers, are celebrated in common in church on Sundays and the more solemn feasts. And the laity, too, are encouraged to recite the Divine Office, either with the priests, or among themselves, or even individually.

101. § 1. In accordance with the centuries-old tradition of the Latin rite, the Latin language is to be retained by clerics in the Divine Office. But in individual cases the ordinary has the power of granting the use of a vernacular translation to those clerics for whom the use of Latin constitutes a grave obstacle to their praying the office properly. The vernacular version, however, must be one that is drawn up according to the provision of Art. 36.

§ 2. The competent superior has the power to grant the use of the vernacular in the celebration of the Divine Office, even in choir, to nuns and to members of institutes dedicated to acquiring perfection, both men who are not clerics and women. The version, however, must be one that is approved.

§ 3. Any cleric bound to the Divine Office fulfils his obligation if he prays the office in the vernacular together with a group of the faithful or with those mentioned in 52 above provided that the text of the translation is approved.

CHAPTER V
THE LITURGICAL YEAR

102. Holy Mother Church is conscious that she must celebrate the saving work of her divine Spouse by devoutly recalling it on certain days throughout the course of the year. Every week, on the day which she has called the Lord's day, she keeps the memory of the Lord's resurrection, which she also celebrates once in the year, together with His blessed passion, in the most solemn festival of Easter.

Within the cycle of a year, moreover, she unfolds the whole mystery of Christ, from the incarnation and birth until the ascension, the day of Pentecost, and the expectation of blessed hope and of the coming of the Lord.

Recalling thus the mysteries of redemption, the Church opens to the faithful the riches of her Lord's powers and merits, so that these are in some way made present for all time, and the faithful are enabled to lay hold upon them and become filled with saving grace.

103. In celebrating this annual cycle of Christ's mysteries, holy Church honours with especial love the Blessed Mary, Mother of God, who is joined by an inseparable bond to the saving work of her Son. In her the Church holds up and admires the most excellent fruit of the redemption, and joyfully contemplates, as in a faultless image, that which she herself desires and hopes wholly to be.

104. The Church has also included in the annual cycle days devoted to the memory of the martyrs and the other saints. Raised up to perfection by the manifold grace of God, and already in possession of eternal salvation, they sing God's perfect praise in heaven and offer prayers for us. By celebrating the passage of these saints from earth to heaven the Church proclaims the Paschal Mystery achieved in the saints who have suffered and been glorified with Christ; she proposes them to the

faithful as examples drawing all to the Father through Christ, and through their merits she pleads for God's favours.

105. Finally, in the various seasons of the year and according to her traditional discipline, the Church completes the formation of the faithful by means of pious practices for soul and body, by instruction, prayer, and works of penance and of mercy.

Accordingly the Sacred Council has seen fit to decree as follows.

106. By a tradition handed down from the apostles which took its origin from the very day of Christ's resurrection, the Church celebrates the Paschal Mystery every eighth day; with good reason this, then, bears the name of the Lord's day or Sunday. For on this day Christ's faithful are bound to come together into one place so that; by hearing the word of God and taking part in the eucharist, they may call to mind the passion, the resurrection and the glorification of the Lord Jesus, and may thank God who "has begotten them again, through the resurrection of Jesus Christ from the dead, unto a living hope" (1 Pet. 1:3). Hence the Lord's day is the original feast day, and it should be proposed to the piety of the faithful and taught to them so that it may become in fact a day of joy and of freedom from work. Other celebrations, unless they be truly of greatest importance, shall not have precedence over the Sunday which is the foundation and kernel of the whole liturgical year.

107. The liturgical year is to be revised so that the traditional customs and discipline of the sacred seasons shall be preserved or restored to suit the conditions of modern times; their specific character is to be retained, so that they duly nourish the piety of the faithful who celebrate the mysteries of Christian redemption, and above all the Paschal Mystery. If certain adaptations are considered necessary on account of local conditions, they are to be made in accordance with the provisions of Art. 39 and 40.

108. The minds of the faithful must be directed primarily toward the feasts of the Lord whereby the mysteries of salvation are celebrated in the course of the year. Therefore, the proper of the

time shall be given the preference which is its due over the feasts of the saints, so that the entire cycle of the mysteries of salvation may be suitably recalled.

109. The season of Lent has a twofold character: primarily by recalling or preparing for baptism and by penance, it disposes the faithful, who more diligently hear the word of God and devote themselves to prayer, to celebrate the Paschal Mystery. This twofold character is to be brought into greater prominence both in the liturgy and by liturgical catechesis. Hence:

    a) More use is to be made of the baptismal features proper to the Lenten liturgy; some of them, which used to flourish in bygone days, are to be restored as may seem good.

    b) The same is to apply to the penitential elements. As regards instruction it is important to impress on the minds of the faithful not only the social consequences of sin but also that essence of the virtue of penance which leads to the detestation of sin as an offence against God; the role of the Church in penitential practices is not to be passed over, and the people must be exhorted to pray for sinners.

110. During Lent penance should not be only internal and individual, but also external and social. The practice of penance should be fostered in ways that are possible in our own times and in different regions, and according to the circumstances of the faithful; it should be encouraged by the authorities mentioned in Art. 22.

    Nevertheless, let the paschal fast be kept sacred. Let it be celebrated everywhere on Good Friday and, where possible, prolonged throughout Holy Saturday, so that the joys of the Sunday of the Resurrection may be attained with uplifted and clear mind.

111. The saints have been traditionally honoured in the Church and their authentic relics and images held in veneration. For the feasts of the saints proclaim the wonderful works of Christ in His

servants, and display to the faithful fitting examples for their imitation.

Lest the feasts of the saints should take precedence over the feasts which commemorate the very mysteries of salvation, many of them should be left to be celebrated by a particular Church or nation or family of religious; only those should be extended to the universal Church which commemorate saints who are truly of universal importance.

CHAPTER VI
SACRED MUSIC

112. The musical tradition of the universal Church is a treasure of inestimable value, greater even than that of any other art. The main reason for this pre-eminence is that, as sacred song united to the words, it forms a necessary or integral part of the solemn liturgy.

Holy Scripture, indeed, has bestowed praise upon sacred song,[42] and the same may be said of the fathers of the Church and of the Roman pontiffs who in recent times, led by St Pius X, have explained more precisely the ministerial function supplied by sacred music in the service of the Lord.

Therefore sacred music is to be considered the more holy in proportion as it is more closely connected with the liturgical action, whether it adds delight to prayer, fosters unity of minds, or confers greater solemnity upon the sacred rites. But the Church approves of all forms of true art having the needed qualities, and admits them into divine worship.

Accordingly, the Sacred Council, keeping to the norms and precepts of ecclesiastical tradition and discipline, and having regard to the purpose of sacred music, which is the glory of God and the sanctification of the faithful, decrees as follows.

113. Liturgical worship is given a more noble form when the divine offices are celebrated solemnly in song, with the assistance of sacred ministers and the active participation of the people.

As regards the language to be used, the provisions of Art. 36 are to be observed; for the Mass, Art. 54; for the sacraments, Art. 63; for the Divine Office, Art. 101.

114. The treasure of sacred music is to be preserved and fostered with great care. Choirs must be diligently promoted, especially in cathedral churches; but bishops and other pastors of souls must be at pains to ensure that, whenever the sacred action is to be

---

[42] Cf. Eph. 5:19; Col. 3:16.

celebrated with song, the whole body of the faithful may be able to contribute that active participation which is rightly theirs, as laid down in Art. 28 and 30.

115. Great importance is to be attached to the teaching and practice of music in seminaries, in the noviciates and houses of study of religious of both sexes, and also in other Catholic institutions and schools. To impart this instruction, teachers are to be carefully trained and put in charge of the teaching of sacred music.

It is desirable also to found higher institutes of sacred music whenever this can be done.

Composers and singers, especially boys, must also be given a genuine liturgical training.

116. The Church acknowledges Gregorian chant as specially suited to the Roman liturgy: therefore, other things being equal, it should be given pride of place in liturgical services.

But other kinds of sacred music, especially polyphony, are by no means excluded from liturgical celebrations, so long as they accord with the spirit of the liturgical action, as laid down in Art. 30.

117. The typical edition of the books of Gregorian chant is to be completed; and a more critical edition is to be prepared of those books already published since the restoration by St Pius X.

It is desirable also that an edition be prepared containing simpler melodies, for use in small churches.

118. Religious singing by the people is to be intelligently fostered so that in devotions and sacred exercises, as also during liturgical services, the voices of the faithful may ring out according to the norms and requirements of the rubrics.

119. In certain parts of the world, especially mission lands, there are peoples who have their own musical traditions, and these play a great part in their religious and social life. For this reason due importance is to be attached to their music, and a suitable place is to be given to it, not only in forming their attitude toward

religion, but also in adapting worship to their native genius, as indicated in Art. 39 and 40.

Therefore, when missionaries are being given training in music, every effort should be made to see that they become competent in promoting the traditional music of these peoples, both in schools and in sacred services, as far as may be practicable.

120. In the Latin Church the pipe organ is to be held in high esteem, for it is the traditional musical instrument which adds a wonderful splendour to the Church's ceremonies and powerfully lifts up man's mind to God and to higher things.

But other instruments also may be admitted for use in divine worship, with the knowledge and consent of the competent territorial authority, as laid down in Art. 22: 2; 37, and 40. This may be done, however, only on condition that the instruments are suitable, or can be made suitable, for sacred use, accord with the dignity of the temple, and truly contribute to the edification of the faithful.

121. Composers, filled with the Christian spirit, should feel that their vocation is to cultivate sacred music and increase its store of treasures.

Let them produce compositions which have the qualities proper to genuine sacred music, not confining themselves to works which can be sung only by large choirs, but providing also for the needs of small choirs and for the active participation of the entire assembly of the faithful.

The texts intended to be sung must always be in conformity with Catholic doctrine; indeed they should be drawn chiefly from holy scripture and from liturgical sources.

CHAPTER VII
SACRED ART AND SACRED FURNISHINGS

122. Very rightly the fine arts are considered to rank among the noblest activities of man's genius, and this applies especially to religious art and to its highest achievement, which is sacred art. These arts, by their very nature, are oriented toward the infinite beauty of God which they attempt in some way to portray by the work of human hands; they achieve their purpose of redounding to God's praise and glory in proportion as they are directed the more exclusively to the single aim of turning men's minds devoutly toward God.

Holy Mother Church has therefore always been the friend of the fine arts and has ever sought their noble help, with the special aim that all things set apart for use in divine worship should be truly worthy, becoming, and beautiful, signs and symbols of the supernatural world, and for this purpose she has trained artists. In fact, the Church has, with good reason, always reserved to herself the right to pass judgement upon the arts, deciding which of the works of artists are in accordance with faith, piety, and cherished traditional laws, and thereby fitted for sacred use.

The Church has been particularly careful to see that sacred furnishings should worthily and beautifully serve the dignity of worship, and has admitted changes in materials, style, or ornamentation prompted by the progress of the technical arts with the passage of time.

Wherefore it has pleased the Fathers to issue the following decrees on these matters.

123. The Church has not adopted any particular style of art as her very own; she has admitted styles from every period according to the natural talents and circumstances of peoples, and the needs of the various rites. Thus, in the course of the centuries, she has brought into being a treasury of art which must be very carefully preserved. The art of our own days, coming from every race and region, shall also be given free scope in the Church, provided that

it adorns the sacred buildings and holy rites with due reverence and honour; thereby it is enabled to contribute its own voice to that wonderful chorus of praise in honour of the Catholic faith sung by great men in times gone by.

124. Ordinaries, by the encouragement and favour they show to art which is truly sacred, should strive after noble beauty rather than mere sumptuous display. This principle is to apply also in the matter of sacred vestments and ornaments.

Let bishops carefully remove from the house of God and from other sacred places those works of artists which are repugnant to faith, morals, and Christian piety, and which offend true religious sense either by depraved forms or by lack of artistic worth, mediocrity and pretence.

And when churches are to be built, let great care be taken that they be suitable for the celebration of liturgical services and for the active participation of the faithful.

125. The practice of placing sacred images in churches so that they may be venerated by the faithful is to be maintained. Nevertheless their number should be moderate and their relative positions should reflect right order. For otherwise they may create confusion among the Christian people and foster devotion of doubtful orthodoxy.

126. When passing judgement on works of art, local ordinaries shall give a hearing to the diocesan commission on sacred art and, if needed, also to others who are especially expert, and to the commissions referred to in Art. 44, 45, and 46.

Ordinaries must be very careful to see that sacred furnishings and works of value are not disposed of or dispersed; for they are the ornaments of the house of God.

127. Bishops should have a special concern for artists, so as to imbue them with the spirit of sacred art and of the Sacred Liturgy. This they may do in person or through suitable priests who are gifted with a knowledge and love of art.

It is also desirable that schools or academies of sacred art should be founded in those parts of the world where they would be useful, so that artists may be trained.

All artists who, prompted by their talents, desire to serve God's glory in holy Church, should ever bear in mind that they are engaged in a kind of sacred imitation of God the Creator, and are concerned with works destined to be used in Catholic worship, to edify the faithful, and to foster their piety and their religious formation.

128. Along with the revision of the liturgical books, as laid down in Art. 25, there is to be an early revision of the canons and ecclesiastical statutes which govern the provision of material things involved in sacred worship. These laws refer especially to the worthy and well planned construction of sacred buildings, the shape and construction of altars, the nobility, placing, and safety of the eucharistic tabernacle, the dignity and suitability of the baptistery, the proper ordering of sacred images, embellishments, and vestments. Laws which seem less suited to the reformed liturgy are to be brought into harmony with it, or else abolished; and any which are helpful are to be retained if already in use, or introduced where they are lacking.

According to the norm of Art. 22 of this Constitution, the territorial bodies of bishops are empowered to adapt such things to the needs and customs of their different regions; this applies especially to the materials and form of sacred furnishings and vestments.

129. During their philosophical and theological studies, clerics are to be taught about the history and development of sacred art, and about the sound principles governing the production of its works. In consequence they will be able to appreciate and preserve the Church's venerable monuments, and be in a position to aid, by good advice, artists who are engaged in producing works of art.

130. It is fitting that the use of pontificals be reserved to those ecclesiastical persons who have episcopal rank or some particular jurisdiction.

APPENDIX
A DECLARATION OF THE SECOND ECUMENICAL COUNCIL OF THE VATICAN ON REVISION OF THE CALENDAR

The Second Ecumenical Sacred Council of the Vatican, recognising the importance of the wishes expressed by many concerning the assignment of the feast of Easter to a fixed Sunday and concerning an unchanging calendar, having carefully considered the effects which could result from the introduction of a new calendar, declares as follows:

1. The Sacred Council would not object if the feast of Easter were assigned to a particular Sunday of the Gregorian Calendar, provided that those whom it may concern, especially the brethren who are not in communion with the Apostolic See, give their assent.
2. The Sacred Council likewise declares that it does not oppose efforts designed to introduce a perpetual calendar into civil society.

But among the various systems which are being suggested to stabilise a perpetual calendar and to introduce it into civil life, the Church has no objection only in the case of those systems which retain and safeguard a seven-day week with Sunday, without the introduction of any days outside the week, so that the succession of weeks may be left intact, unless there is question of the most serious reasons. Concerning these the Apostolic See shall judge.

The Benedictine Abbey
of Saint Michael at Farnborough
was founded from the French
Abbey of Solesmes in 1895. The monks live
a traditional life of prayer, work and study
in accordance with the ancient
Rule of Saint Benedict.
At the heart of their life is the praise of God
expressed through the solemn
celebration of the Sacred Liturgy,
and supported through their work,
of which this publication is an example.